A SUMMARY OF
CHRISTIAN
DOCTRINE

A SUMMARY OF CHRISTIAN DOCTRINE

Louis Berkhof

THE BANNER OF TRUTH TRUST

THE BANNER OF TRUTH TRUST
3 Murrayfield Road, Edinburgh EH12 6EL, UK

*

© Louis Berkhof 1938
British edition by kind permission of
Wm. B. Eerdmans Publishing Co., USA

First impression 1960
Reprinted 1962
Reprinted 1968
Reprinted 1971
Reprinted 1974
Reprinted 1978
Reprinted 1985
Reprinted 1993
Reprinted 1997
Reprinted 2000
Reprinted 2002
This reset edition 2005
Reprinted 2009

ISBN-13: 978 0 85151 055 2

All Scripture quotations are from the
American Standard Version, 1901

*

Typeset in 11 / 14 pt Adobe Caslon Pro
at the Banner of Truth Trust

Printed in the U.S.A. by
Versa Press, Inc.,
East Peoria, IL

CONTENTS

The Doctrine of the Application of the Work of Redemption

The Doctrine of the Church and the Means of Grace

The Doctrine of the Last Things

INTRODUCTION

I

Religion

1. THE NATURE OF RELIGION. The Bible informs us that man was created in the image of God. When he fell in sin, he did not entirely cease to be the image-bearer of the Most High. The seed of religion is still present in all men, though their sinful nature constantly reacts against it. Missionaries testify to the presence of religion in some form or other among all the nations and tribes of the earth. It is one of the greatest blessings of mankind, though many denounce it as a curse. Not only does it touch the deepest springs of man's life, but it also controls his thoughts and feelings and desires.

But just what is religion? It is only by the study of the Word of God that we can learn to know the nature of true religion. The word 'religion' is derived from the Latin and not from any word that is found in the original Hebrew or Greek of the Bible. It is found only four times in our translation of the Bible, *Gal* 1:13, 14; *James* 1:26, 27. The Old Testament defines religion as the fear of the Lord. This fear is not a feeling of dread, but of reverent regard for God akin to awe, but coupled with love and confidence. It is the response of the Old Testament believers to the revelation of the law. In the New Testament religion is a response to the gospel rather than to the law, and assumes the form of faith and godliness.

In the light of Scripture we learn to understand that religion is a relation in which man stands to God, a relation in which man is conscious of the absolute majesty and infinite power of God and of his own utter insignificance and absolute helplessness. It may be defined as *a conscious and voluntary relationship to God, which expresses itself*

I

in grateful worship and loving service. The manner of this religious worship and service is not left to the arbitrary will of man, but is determined by God.

2.   THE SEAT OF RELIGION. There are several wrong views respecting the seat of religion in man. Some think of religion primarily as a sort of knowledge, and locate it in the intellect. Others regard it as a kind of immediate feeling of God, and find its seat in the feelings. And still others hold that it consists most of all in moral activity, and refer it to the will. However, all these views are one-sided and contrary to Scripture, which teaches us that religion is a matter of the heart. In Scripture psychology the heart is the central organ of the soul. Out of it are all the issues of life, thoughts, feelings, and desires, *Prov.* 4:23. Religion involves the whole man, his intellectual, his emotional, and his moral life. This is the only view that does justice to the nature of religion.

3.   THE ORIGIN OF RELIGION. Particular attention was devoted during the last fifty years to the problem of the origin of religion. Repeated attempts were made to give a natural explanation of it, but without success. Some spoke of it as an invention of cunning and deceptive priests, who regarded it as an easy source of revenue; but this explanation is entirely discredited now. Others held that it began with the worship of lifeless objects (fetishes), or with the worship of spirits, possibly the spirits of forefathers. But this is no explanation, since the question remains, How did people ever hit upon the idea of *worshipping* lifeless or living objects? Still others were of the opinion that religion originated in nature-worship, that is, the worship of the marvels and powers of nature, or in the widespread practice of magic. But these theories do not explain any more than the others how non-religious man ever became religious. They all start out with a man who is already religious.

The Bible gives the only reliable account of the origin of religion. It informs us of the existence of God, the only object worthy of religious worship. Moreover, it comes to us with the assurance that God, whom man could never discover with his natural powers, revealed Himself in nature and, more especially, in His divine Word, demands the worship and service of man, and also determines the worship and service that is well-pleasing to Him. And, finally, it teaches us that God created man in His own image, and thus endowed him with a capacity to understand, and to respond to, this revelation, and engendered in him a natural urge to seek communion with God and to glorify Him.

To memorize. Scripture passages bearing on:

a. *The Nature of Religion*:

Deut. 10:12, 13. 'And now, Israel, what doth Jehovah thy God require of thee, but to fear Jehovah thy God, to walk in all His ways, and to love Him, and to serve Jehovah thy God with all thy heart and with all thy soul, to keep the commandments of Jehovah, and His statutes which I command thee this day for thy good?'

Psa. 111:10. 'The fear of Jehovah is the beginning of wisdom; a good understanding have all they that do His commandments: His praise endureth for ever.'

Eccles. 12:13. 'Fear God and keep His commandments; for this is the whole duty of man.'

John 6:29. 'This is the work of God, that ye believe on Him whom He hath sent.'

Acts 16:31. 'And they said, Believe on the Lord Jesus, and thou shalt be saved, thou and thy house.'

b. *The Seat of Religion*:

Psa. 51:10. 'Create in me a clean heart, O God; and renew a right spirit within me.' Also verse 17. 'The sacrifices of God are a broken spirit; a broken and a contrite heart, O God, thou wilt not despise.'

Prov. 4:23. 'Keep thy heart with all diligence; for out of it are the issues of life.'

Matt. 5:8. 'Blessed are the pure in heart: for they shall see God.'

c. *The Origin of Religion*:

Gen. 1:27. 'And God created man in His own image, in the image of God created He him.'

Deut. 4:13. 'And He declared unto you His covenant, which He commanded you to perform, even the ten commandments.'

Ezek. 36:26. 'A new heart also will I give you, and a new spirit will I put within you; and I will take away the stony heart out of your flesh, and I will give you a heart of flesh.'

For Further Study of Scripture:

a.   What elements of true religion are indicated in the following passages? *Deut.* 10:12; *Eccles.* 12:13; *Hos.* 6:6; *Mic.* 6:8; *Mark* 12:33; *John* 3:36; 6:29; *Acts* 6:3; *Rom.* 12:1; 13:10; *James* 1:27.

b.   What forms of false religion are indicated in the following passages? *Psa.* 78:35, 36; *Isa.* 1:11–17; 58:1–5; *Ezek.* 33:31, 32; *Matt.* 6:2, 5; 7:21, 26, 27; 23:14; *Luke* 6:2; 13:14; *Gal.* 4:10; *Col.* 2:20; *2 Tim.* 3:5; *Titus* 1:16; *James* 2:15, 16; 3:10.

c.   Name six instances of true religion. *Gen.* 4:4–8; 12:1–8; 15:17; 18:22–33; *Exod.* 3:2–22; *Deut.* 32:33; *2 Kings* 18:3–7; 19:14–19; *Dan.* 6:4–22; *Luke* 2:25–35; 2:36, 37; 7:1–10; *2 Tim.* 1:5.

Questions for Review:

1.   Is religion limited to certain tribes and nations?
2.   How can we learn to know the real nature of true religion?
3.   What terms are used in the Old and New Testament to describe religion?
4.   How would you define religion?
5.   What mistaken notions are there as to the seat of religion in man?
6.   What is the centre of the religious life according to Scripture?
7.   What different explanations have been given of the origin of religion?
8.   What is the only satisfactory explanation?

2

Revelation

1. REVELATION IN GENERAL. The discussion of religion naturally leads on to that of revelation as its origin. If God had not revealed himself, religion would have been impossible. Man could not possibly have had any knowledge of God, if God had not made Himself known. Left to himself, he would never have discovered God. We distinguish between God's revelation in nature and His revelation in Scripture.

Atheists and Agnostics, of course, do not believe in revelation. Pantheists sometimes speak of it, though there is really no place for it in their system of thought. And Deists admit the revelation of God in nature, but deny the necessity, the reality, and even the possibility of any special revelation such as we have in Scripture. We believe in both general and special revelation.

2. GENERAL REVELATION. The general revelation of God is prior to His special revelation in point of time. It does not come to man in the form of verbal communications, but in the facts, the forces, and the laws of nature, in the constitution and operation of the human mind, and in the facts of experience and history.

The Bible refers to it in such passages as *Psa.* 19:1, 2; *Rom.* 1:19, 20; 2:14, 15.

a. *Insufficiency of general revelation.* While Pelagians, Rationalists, and Deists regard this revelation as adequate for our present needs, Roman Catholics and Protestants are agreed that it is not sufficient. It was obscured by the blight of sin resting on God's beautiful creation. The handwriting of the Creator was not entirely erased, but became hazy and indistinct. It does not now convey any fully reliable knowledge of God and spiritual things and therefore does not furnish us a trustworthy foundation on which we can build for our eternal future. The present religious confusion of those who would base their religion on a purely natural basis clearly proves its insufficiency. It does not even afford an adequate basis for religion in general, much less for true religion. Even Gentile nations appeal to some supposed special revelation. And finally it utterly fails to meet the spiritual needs of sinners. While it conveys some knowledge of the goodness, the wisdom, and the power of God, it conveys no knowledge whatever of Christ as the only way of salvation.

b. *Value of general revelation.* This does not mean, however, that general revelation has no value at all. It accounts for the true elements that are still found in heathen religions. Due to this revelation Gentiles feel themselves to be the offspring of God, *Acts* 17:28, seek after God if haply they might find Him, *Acts* 17:27, see in nature God's everlasting power and divinity, *Rom.* 1:19, 20, and do by nature the things of the law, *Rom.* 2:14. Though they live in the darkness of sin and ignorance, and pervert the truth of God, they still share in the illumination of the Word, *John* 1:9, and in the general operations of the Holy Spirit, *Gen.* 6:3. Moreover, the general revelation of God also forms the background for His special revelation. The latter could not be fully understood without the former. Science and history do not fail to illumine the pages of the Bible.

3.   SPECIAL REVELATION. In addition to the revelation of God in nature we have His special revelation which is now embodied in Scripture. The Bible is pre-eminently the book of God's special revelation, a revelation in which facts and words go hand in hand, the words interpreting the facts and the facts giving substance to the words.

a. *Necessity of special revelation.* This revelation became necessary through the entrance of sin into the world. God's handwriting in nature was obscured and corrupted, and man was stricken with spiritual blindness, became subject to error and unbelief, and now in his blindness and perverseness fails to read aright even the remaining traces of the original revelation, and is unable to understand any further revelation of God. Therefore it became necessary that God should reinterpret the truths of nature, should provide a new revelation of redemption, and should illumine the mind of man and redeem it from the power of error.

b. *Means of special revelation.* In giving His special or supernatural revelation God used different kinds of means, such as (1) *Theophanies or visible manifestations of God.* He revealed His presence in fire and clouds of smoke, *Exod.* 3:2; 33:9; *Psa.* 78:14; 99:7; in stormy winds, *Job* 38:1; *Psa.* 18:10–16, and in a 'still small voice,' *1 Kings* 19.12. These were all tokens of His presence, revealing something of His glory. Among the Old Testament appearances those of the Angel of Jehovah, the second Person of the Trinity, occupied a prominent place, *Gen.* 16:13; 31:11; *Exod.* 23:20–23; *Mal.* 3:1. The highest point of the personal appearance of God among men was reached in the incarnation of Jesus Christ. In Him the Word became flesh and tabernacled among us, *John* 1:14.

(2) *Direct communications.* Sometimes God spoke to men in an audible voice, as He did to Moses and the children of Israel, *Deut.* 5:4, and sometimes He suggested His messages to the prophets by an internal operation of the Holy Spirit, *1 Pet.* 1:11. Moreover, He revealed Himself in dreams and visions, and by means of Urim and Thummim, *Num.*12:6; 27:21; *Isa.* 6. And in the New Testament Christ appears as the great Teacher sent from God to reveal the Father's will; and through His Spirit the apostles become the organs of further revelations, *John* 14:26; *1 Cor.* 2:12, 13; *1 Thess.* 2:13.

(3) *Miracles.* The miracles of the Bible should never be regarded as mere marvels which fill men with amazement, but as essential parts of God's special revelation. They are manifestations of the special power of God, tokens of His special presence, and often serve to symbolize spiritual truths. They are signs of the coming Kingdom of God and of the redemptive power of God. The greatest miracle of all is the coming of the Son of God in the flesh. In Him the whole creation of God is being restored and brought back to its original beauty, *1 Tim.* 3:16; *Rev.* 21:5.

c. *The character of special revelation.* This special revelation of God is a revelation of redemption. It reveals the plan of God for the redemption of sinners and of the world, and the way in which this plan is realized. It is instrumental in renewing man; it illumines his mind and inclines his will to that which is good; it fills him with holy affections, and prepares him for his heavenly home. Not only does it bring us a message of redemption; it also acquaints us with redemptive facts. It not only enriches us with knowledge, but also transforms lives by changing sinners into saints. This revelation is clearly progressive. The great truths of redemption appear but dimly at first but gradually increase in clearness, and finally stand out in the New Testament in all their fulness and beauty.

To memorize. Scripture passages bearing on:

a. *General Revelation:*
Psa. 8:1. 'O Jehovah, our Lord, how excellent is Thy name in all the earth.'
Psa. 19:1, 2. 'The heavens declare the glory of God; and the firmament showeth His handiwork. Day unto day uttereth speech, and night unto night showeth wisdom.'
Rom. 1:20. 'For the invisible things of Him since the creation of the world are clearly seen, being perceived through the things that are made, even His everlasting power and divinity.'
Rom. 2:14, 15. 'For when Gentiles that have not the law do by nature the things of the law, these, not having the law, are a law unto themselves; in that they show the work of the law written in their hearts, their consciences bearing witness therewith, and their thoughts one with another accusing or else excusing them.'

b. *Special Revelation:*
Num. 12:6–8. 'And He said, Hear now my words: if there be a prophet among you, I Jehovah will make myself known unto him in a vision, I will speak with him in a dream. My servant Moses is not so; he is faithful in all my house: with him will I speak mouth to mouth.'
Heb. 1:1. 'God having of old time spoken unto the fathers in the prophets by divers portions and in divers manners, hath at the end of these days spoken unto us in His Son.'
2 Pet. 1:21. 'For no prophecy ever came by the will of man: but men spake from God, being moved by the Holy Spirit.'

For Further Study:

a. Mention some of the appearances of the Angel or Jehovah. Can he have been a mere angel? *Gen.* 16:13; 31:11, 13; 32:28; *Exod.* 23:20.23.

b. Name some examples or revelation by dreams. *Gen.* 28:10–17; 31:24; 41:2–7; *Judg.* 7.13; *1 Kings* 3:5–9; *Dan.* 2:1–3; *Matt.* 2:13,19,20.

c. Mention some cases in which God revealed Himself in visions. *Isa.* 6; *Ezek.* 1–3; *Dan.* 2:19; 7:1–14; *Zech.* 2–6.

d. Can you infer from the following passages what the miracles recorded reveal? *Exod.* 10:1, 2; *Deut.* 8:3; *John* 2:1–11; 6:1–14, 25–35; 9:1–7; 11:17–44.

Questions for Review:

1. How do general and special revelations differ?
2. Where do we meet with the denial of all revelation of God?
3. What is the position of the Deists as to revelation?
4. What is the nature of general revelation?
5. Why is it insufficient for our special needs, and what value does it have?
6. Why was God's special revelation necessary?
7. What means did God employ in His special revelation?
8. What are the characteristics of special revelation?

3
Scripture

1.   REVELATION AND SCRIPTURE. The term 'special revelation' may be used in more than one sense. It may denote the direct
self-communications of God in verbal messages and in miraculous facts.
The prophets and the apostles often received messages from God long
before they committed them to writing. These are now contained in
Scripture, but do not constitute the whole of the Bible. There is much
in it that was not revealed in a supernatural way, but is the result of
study and of previous reflection. However, the term may also be used to
denote the Bible as a whole, that whole complex of redemptive truths
and facts, with the proper historical setting, that is found in Scripture
and has the divine guarantee of its truth in the fact that it is infallibly
inspired by the Holy Spirit. In view of this fact it may be said that the
whole Bible, and the Bible only, is for us God's special revelation. It is
in the Bible that God's special revelation lives on and brings even now
life, light, and holiness.

2.   SCRIPTURE PROOF FOR THE INSPIRATION OF
SCRIPTURE. The whole Bible is given by inspiration of God, and
is as such the infallible rule of faith and practice for all mankind.
Since the doctrine of inspiration is often denied, it calls for special
consideration. This doctrine, like every other, is based on Scripture, and is not an invention of man. While it is founded on a great
number of passages, only a few of these can be indicated here. The
Old Testament writers are repeatedly instructed to write what the
Lord commands them, *Exod.* 17:14; 34:27; *Num.* 33:2; *Isa.* 8:1; 30:8;
Jer. 25:13; 30:2; *Ezek.* 24:1; *Dan.* 12:4; *Hab.* 2:2. The prophets were
conscious of bringing the Word of the Lord, and therefore introduced

their messages with some such formula as, 'Thus saith the Lord,' or, 'The word of the Lord came unto me,' *Jer.* 36:27, 32; *Ezek.* chapters 26, 27, 31, 32, 39. Paul speaks of his words as Spirit-taught words, *1 Cor.* 2:13, claims that Christ is speaking in him, *2 Cor.* 13:3, and describes his message to the Thessalonians as the word of God, *1 Thess.* 2:13. The Epistle to the Hebrews often quotes passages of the Old Testament as words of God or of the Holy Spirit, *Heb.* 1:5; 3:7; 4:3; 5:6; 7:21. The most important passage to prove the inspiration of Scripture is *2 Tim.* 3:16, which reads as follows in the Authorized Version: 'All Scripture is given by inspiration of God, and is profitable for doctrine, for reproof, for correction, for instruction in righteousness.'

3.   THE NATURE OF INSPIRATION. There are especially two wrong views of inspiration, representing extremes that should be avoided.

a.   *Mechanical Inspiration.* It has sometimes been represented as if God literally dictated what the human authors of the Bible had to write, and as if they were purely passive like a pen in the hand of a writer. This means that their minds did not contribute in any way to the contents or form of their writings. But in view of what we find in Scripture this can hardly be true. They were real authors, who in some cases gathered their materials from sources at their command, *1 Kings* 11:41; 14:29; *1 Chron.* 29.29; *Luke* 1:1–4, in other instances recorded their own experiences as, for instance, in many of the psalms, and impressed upon their writings their own particular style. The style of Isaiah differs from that of Jeremiah, and the style of John is not like that of Paul.

b.   *Dynamic Inspiration.* Others thought of the process of inspiration as affecting only the writers, and having no direct bearing on their writings. Their mental and spiritual life was strengthened and raised to a higher pitch, so that they saw things more clearly and had a more profound sense of their real spiritual value. This inspiration was not limited to the time when they wrote the books of the Bible, but was a permanent characteristic of the writers and affected their writings only indirectly. It differed only in degree from the spiritual illumination of all believers. This theory certainly does not do justice to the biblical view of inspiration.

c.   *Organic Inspiration.* The proper conception of inspiration holds that the Holy Spirit acted on the writers of the Bible in an organic way, in harmony with the laws of their own inner being, using them just as they were, with their character and temperament, their gifts and talents, their education and culture, their vocabulary and style. The Holy Spirit illumined their minds, aided their memory, prompted them to write, repressed the influence of sin on their writings, and guided them in the expression of their thoughts even to the choice of their words. In no small measure He left free scope to their own activity. They could give the results of their own investigations, write of their own experiences, and put the imprint of their own style and language on their books.

4.   THE EXTENT OF INSPIRATION. There are differences of opinion also respecting the extent of the inspiration of Scripture.

a. *Partial Inspiration.* Under the influence of Rationalism it has become quite common to deny the inspiration of the Bible altogether, or to hold that only parts of it are inspired. Some deny the inspiration of the Old Testament while admitting that of the New. Others affirm that the moral and religious teachings of Scripture are inspired, but that its historical parts contain several chronological, archaeological, and scientific mistakes. Still others limit the inspiration to the Sermon on the Mount. They who adopt such views have already lost their Bible, for the very differences of opinion are proof positive that no one can determine with any degree of certainty which parts of Scripture are, and which are not, inspired. There is still another way in which the inspiration of Scripture is limited, namely, by assuming that the thoughts were inspired while the choice of the words was left entirely to the wisdom of the human authors. But this proceeds on the very doubtful assumption that the thoughts can be separated from the words, while, as a matter of fact, accurate thought without words is impossible.

b.   *Plenary Inspiration.* According to Scripture every part of the Bible is inspired. Jesus and the apostles frequently appeal to the Old Testament books as 'Scripture' or 'the Scriptures' to settle a point in controversy. To their minds such an appeal was equivalent to an appeal to God. It should be noted that of the books to which they appeal in this fashion, some are historical. The Epistle to the Hebrews repeatedly cites passages from the Old Testament as words of God or of the Holy Spirit (cf. p. 11). Peter places the letters of Paul on a level with the writings of the Old Testament, *2 Pet.* 3:16, and Paul speaks of all Scripture as inspired, *2 Tim.* 3:16.

We may safely go a step farther and say that the inspiration of the Bible extends to the very words employed. The Bible is verbally inspired, which is not equivalent to saying that it is mechanically inspired. The doctrine of verbal inspiration is fully warranted by Scripture. In many cases we are explicitly told that the Lord told Moses and Joshua exactly what to write, *Lev.* 3 and 4; 6:1, 24; 7:22, 28; *Josh.* 1:1; 4:1; 6:2, and so on. The prophets speak of Jehovah as putting His words into their mouths, *Jer.* 1:9, and as directing them to speak His words to the people, *Ezek.* 3:4, 10, 11. Paul designates his words as Spirit-taught words, *1 Cor.* 2:13; and both he and Jesus base an argument on a single word, *Matt.* 22:43–45; *John* 10.35; *Gal.* 3:16.

5.   THE PERFECTIONS OF SCRIPTURE. The Reformers developed the doctrine of Scripture as over against the Roman Catholics and some of the Protestant sects. While Rome taught that the Bible owes its authority to the church, they maintained that it has authority in itself as the inspired Word of God. They also upheld the necessity of Scripture as the divinely appointed means of grace, over against the Roman Catholics, who asserted that the church had no absolute need of it, and some of the Protestant sects, who exalted the 'inner light' or the word of the Holy Spirit in the hearts of the people of God, at the expense of Scripture.

In opposition to Rome they further defended the clearness of the Bible. They did not deny that it contains mysteries too deep for human understanding, but simply contended that the knowledge necessary unto salvation, though not equally clear on every page of the Bible, is yet conveyed in a manner so simple that anyone earnestly seeking salvation can easily gather knowledge for himself, and need not depend on the interpretation of the church or the priesthood.

Finally, they also defended the sufficiency of Scripture, and thereby denied the need of the tradition of the Roman Catholics and of the inner light of the Anabaptists.

To memorize. Passages bearing on:

a. *The inspiration of Scripture.*
1 Cor. 2:13. 'Which things also we speak, not in words which man's wisdom teacheth, but which the Spirit teacheth; combining spiritual things with spiritual words.'
1 Thess. 2:13. 'And for this cause we also thank God without ceasing, that, when ye received from us the word of the message, even the word of God, ye accepted it not as the word of men, but, as it is in truth, the word of God.'
2 Tim. 3:16. 'All Scripture is given by inspiration of God, and is profitable for doctrine, for reproof, for correction, for instruction in righteousness' (AV).

b. *The authority of the Bible:*
Isa. 8:20. 'To the law and to the testimony! if they speak not according to this word, surely there is no morning for them.'

c. *The necessity of the Bible:*
2 Tim. 3:15. 'And that from a babe thou hast known the sacred writings, which are able to make thee wise unto salvation through faith which is in Christ Jesus.'

d. *The clearness of Scripture:*
Psa. 19:7b. 'The testimony of Jehovah is sure; making wise the simple.'
Psa. 119:105. 'Thy word is a lamp unto my feet, and a light unto my path.'
Also verse 130. 'The opening of Thy words giveth light; it giveth understanding to the simple.'

e. *The sufficiency of Scripture:* see the passage under c. above.

For Further Study:
a.   Do the traditions of men have authority? *Matt.* 5:21–48; 15:3–6; *Mark* 7:7; *Col.* 2:8; *Titus* 1:14; *2 Pet.* 1:18.
b.   Did the prophets themselves always fully understand what they wrote? *Dan.* 8:15; 12.8; *Zech.* 1:7–6:11; *1 Pet.* 1:11.
c.   Does *2 Tim.* 3:16 teach us anything respecting the practical value of the inspiration of Scripture? If so, what?

Questions for Review:
1.   What is the relation between special revelation and Scripture?
2.   What different meanings has the term 'special revelation'?
3.   Can we say that special revelation and Scripture are identical?
4.   What Scripture proof can you give for the inspiration of the Bible?
5   What are the theories of mechanical and dynamical inspiration?
6.   How would you describe the doctrine of organic inspiration?
7.   What about the theory that the thoughts are inspired but not the words?
8.   How would you prove that inspiration extends to every part of Scripture, and even to the very words?
9.   How do Rome and the Reformers differ on the authority, the necessity, the clearness, and the sufficiency of Scripture?

4
The Essential Nature of God

1.   THE KNOWLEDGE OF GOD. The possibility of knowing God has been denied on several grounds. But while it is true that man can never fully comprehend God, it does not follow that he can have no knowledge of Him at all. He can know Him only in part, but nevertheless with a knowledge which is real and true. This is possible because God has revealed Himself. Left to his own resources, man would never have been able to discover nor to know Him.

Our knowledge of God is twofold. Man has an *inborn knowledge* of God. This does not merely mean that, in virtue of his creation in the image of God, he has a natural capacity to know God. Neither does it imply that man at birth brings a certain knowledge of God with him into the world. It simply means that under normal conditions a certain knowledge of God naturally develops in man. This knowledge is, of course, of a very general nature.

But in addition to this inborn knowledge of God man also *acquires knowledge* of Him by learning from God's general and special revelation. This is not obtained without efforts on man's part, but is the result of his conscious and sustained pursuit of knowledge. While this knowledge is possible only because man is born with the capacity to know God, it carries him far beyond the limits of the inborn knowledge of God.

2.   THE KNOWLEDGE OF GOD AS KNOWN FROM SPECIAL REVELATION. While it is not possible to define God, it is possible to give a general description of His being. It is perhaps best

to describe Him as a pure Spirit of infinite perfections. The description involves the following elements:

a.   *God is a pure Spirit.* The Bible contains no definition of God. The nearest approach to it is found in the words of Jesus to the Samaritan woman, 'God is spirit.' This means that He is essentially spirit, and that all the qualities which belong to the perfect idea of spirit are necessarily found in Him. The fact that He is pure spirit excludes the idea that He has a body of some kind and is in any way visible to the physical eye.

b.   *God is personal.* The fact that God is spirit also involves His personality. A spirit is an intelligent and moral being, and when we ascribe personality to God, we mean exactly that He is a reasonable being capable of determining the course of His life. At present many deny the personality of God and simply conceive of Him as an impersonal force or power. However, the God of the Bible is certainly a personal God, a God with whom men can converse, whom they can trust, who enters into their experiences, who helps them in their difficulties, and who fills their hearts with joy and gladness. Moreover, He revealed Himself in a personal form in Jesus Christ.

c.   *God is infinitely perfect.* God is distinguished from all His creatures by infinite perfection. His being and virtues are free from all limitations and imperfections. He is not only boundless and limitless, but also stands out above all His creatures in moral perfection and in glorious majesty. The children of Israel sang of the greatness of God after they passed through the Red Sea: 'Who is like unto Thee, O Jehovah, among the gods? Who is like Thee, glorious in holiness, fearful in praise, doing wonders?' (*Exod.* 15:11). Some philosophers of the present day speak of God as 'finite, developing, struggling, suffering, sharing with man his defeats and victory'.

d.   *God and His perfections are one.* Simplicity is one of the fundamental characteristics of God. This means that He is not composed of different parts, and also that His being and attributes are one. It may be said that God's perfections are God Himself as He has revealed Himself to man. They are simply so many manifestations of the divine Being. Hence the Bible says that God is truth, life, light, love, righteousness, and so on.

To memorize. Passages proving:

a. *That God can be known:*
1 John 5:20. 'And we know that the Son of God is come, and hath given us an understanding, that we may know Him that is true, and we are in Him that is true, even in His Son Jesus Christ.'
John 17:3. 'And this is life eternal, that they should know thee, the only true God, and Him whom thou didst send, even Jesus Christ.'

b. *That God is a Spirit:*
John 4:24. 'God is a Spirit: and they that worship Him must worship Him in spirit and in truth.'
1 Tim. 6:16. 'Who only hath immortality, dwelling in light unapproachable; whom no man hath seen, nor can see.'

c. *That God is personal:*
Mal. 2:10. 'Have we not all one father? Hath not one God created us?'
John 14:9b. 'He that hath seen me hath seen the Father; how sayest thou, Show us the Father?'

d. *That God is infinite in perfection:*
Exod. 15:11. 'Who is like unto Thee, O Jehovah, among the gods? Who is like Thee, glorious in holiness, fearful in praises, doing wonders?'
Psa. 147:5. 'Great is our Lord, and mighty in power; His understanding is infinite.'

For Further Study:
a. Do not the following passages teach that we cannot know God? *Job* 11:7; 26:14,136:26.
b. If God is a spirit and has no body, how do you explain the following passages? *Psa.* 4:6; 17:2; 18:6, 8, 9; 31:5; 44:3; 47:8; 48:10, and many others.
c. How do the following passages testify to the personality of God? *Gen.* 1:1; *Deut.* 1:34, 35; *1 Kings* 8:23–26; *Job* 38:1; *Psa.* 21:7; 50:6; 103:3–5; *Matt.* 5:9; *Rom.* 12:1.

Questions for Review:

1. In what sense is God knowable and in what sense unknowable?
2. What is the difference between inborn and acquired knowledge of God?
3. Is it possible to define God? How would you describe Him?
4. What is involved in God's spirituality?
5. What do we mean when we speak of God as a personality?
6. What proof have we for the personality of God?
7. What do we mean when we speak of the infinity of God?
8. How are the being of God and His perfections related?

5

The Names of God

When God gives names to persons or things, they are names which have meaning and give an insight into the nature of the persons or things designated. This also applies to the names which God has given Himself. Sometimes the Bible speaks of the name of God in the singular, and in such cases the term is a designation of the manifestation of God in general, especially in relation to His people, *Exod.* 20:7; *Psa.* 113:3; or simply stands for God Himself, *Prov.* 18:10; *Isa.* 50:10. The one general name of God is split up into several special names, which are expressive of His many-sided being. These names are not of human invention, but are given by God Himself.

1.   THE OLD TESTAMENT NAMES OF GOD. Some of the Old Testament names denote that God is the High and Exalted One. *'El* and *'Elohim* indicate that He is strong and mighty and should therefore be feared, while *'Elyon* points to His exalted nature as the Most High, the object of reverence and worship. Another name belonging to this class is *'Adonai*, usually rendered 'Lord', the Possessor and Ruler of all men. Other names express the fact that God enters into relations of friendship with His creatures. One of these, common among the patriarchs, was the name *Shaddai* or *'El-Shaddai*, which indeed stresses the divine greatness, but as a source of comfort and blessing for His people. It indicates that God controls the powers of nature, and makes them serve His purposes. The greatest name of God, however, always held sacred by the Jew, is the name *Jehovah (Yahweh)*. Its origin and meaning is indicated in *Exod.* 3:14, 15. It expresses the fact that God is always the same, and especially that He is unchangeable in His covenant relationship, and is always faithful in the fulfilment of His promises. It frequently assumes a fuller form in 'Jehovah of Hosts'.

This calls up the picture of Jehovah as the King of Glory surrounded by angelic hosts.

2.   THE NEW TESTAMENT NAMES OF GOD. The New Testament names are simply the Greek forms of those found in the Old Testament. The following deserve particular attention:

a.   *The name Theos.* This is simply the word for 'God', and is the most common name employed in the New Testament. It is frequently found with a possessive genitive as 'my God', 'thy God', 'our God', 'your God'. In Christ, God is the God of each one of His children. The individual form takes the place of the national form, 'the God of Israel', so common in the Old Testament.

b.   *The name Kurios.* This is the word for 'Lord', a name that is applied not only to God but also to Christ. It takes the place of both *'Adonai* and *Jehovah*, though its meaning corresponds more particularly with that of *'Adonai*. It designates God as the Possessor and Ruler of all things, and especially of His people.

c.   *The name Pater.* It is often said that the New Testament introduced this as a new name. But this is hardly correct, for the name 'Father' is also found in the Old Testament to express the special relation in which God stands to Israel, *Deut.* 32:6; *Isa.* 63:16. In the New Testament it is more individual in that it points to God as the Father of all believers. Sometimes it designates God as the Creator of all, *1 Cor.* 8:6; *Eph.* 3:14; *Heb.* 12:9; *James* 1:17, and sometimes the first Person of the Trinity as the Father of Christ, *John* 14:11; 17.1.

To memorize. Passages bearing on:

a. *The name of God in general:*
Exod. 20:7. 'Thou shalt not take the name of Jehovah thy God in vain; for Jehovah will not hold him guiltless that taketh His name in vain.'
Psa. 8:1. 'O Jehovah, our Lord, how excellent is Thy name in all the earth!'

b. *Particular names:*
Gen. 1:1. 'In the beginning God (*'Elohim*) created the heavens and the earth.'

Exod. 6:3. 'And I appeared unto Abraham, unto Isaac, and unto Jacob, as God Almighty (*'El-Shaddai*); but by my name Jehovah I was not known unto them.'

Psa. 86:8. 'There is none like Thee among the gods, O Lord (*'Adonai*); neither are there any works like unto Thy works.'

Mal. 3:6. 'For I, Jehovah, change not; therefore ye, O sons of Jacob, are not consumed.'

Matt. 6:9. 'Our Father who art in Heaven, Hallowed be Thy name.'

Rev. 4:8. 'Holy, holy, holy, is the Lord (Kurios) God, the Almighty, who was and who is and who is to come.'

For Further Study:

a. What light does *Exod.* 3:13–16 shed on the meaning of the name *Jehovah*?

b. What name of God was rather common in the times of the patriarchs? *Gen.* 17:1; 28:3; 35:11; 43:14; 48:3; 49:25; *Exod.* 6:3.

c. Can you give some descriptive names of God? *Isa.* 43:3, 15; 44:6; *Amos* 4:13; *Luke* 1:78; *2 Cor.* 1:3; 11:31; *James* 1:17; *Heb.* 12:9; *Rev.* 1:8, 17.

Questions for Review:

1. What does Scripture mean when it speaks of the name of God in the singular?

2. Are the special names of God of human origin?

3. What two kinds of names do we distinguish in the Old Testament?

4. What is the meaning of the names *'Elohim, Jehovah, 'Adonai, 'El-Shaddai* and *Kurios*?

5. Is the name *Father* ever applied to God in the Old Testament?

6. In what different senses is this name used in the New Testament?

6

The Attributes of God

God reveals Himself not only in His names, but also in His attributes, that is, in the perfections of the divine Being. It is customary to distinguish between incommunicable and communicable attributes. Of the former there are no traces in the creature; of the latter there are.

1.   THE INCOMMUNICABLE ATTRIBUTES. These emphasize the absolute distinction between God and the creature, and include the following:

a.   *The independence or self-existence of God.* This means that God has the ground of His existence in Himself and, unlike man, does not depend on anything outside of Himself. He is independent in His Being, in His virtues and actions, and independence causes all His creatures to depend on Him. The idea is embodied in the name Jehovah and finds expression in the following passages, *Psa.* 33:11; 115:3; *Isa.* 40:18 ff.; *Dan.* 4:35; *John* 5:26; *Rom.* 11:33–36; *Acts* 17:25; *Rev.* 4:11.

b.   *The immutability of God.* Scripture teaches that God is unchangeable. He is forever the same in His divine Being and perfections, and also in His purposes and promises, *Num.* 23:19; *Psa.* 33:11; 102:27; *Mal.* 3:6; *Heb.* 6:17; *James* 1:17. This does not mean, however, that there is no movement in God. The Bible speaks of Him as coming and going, hiding and revealing Himself. He. is also said to repent, but this is evidently only a human way of speaking of God, *Exod.* 32:14; *Jonah* 3.10, and really indicates a change in man's relation to God.

c.   *The infinity of God.* This means that *God is not subject to limitations.* We can speak of His infinity in more than one sense. Viewed in relation to His being, it may be called His *absolute perfection.* He is unlimited in His knowledge and wisdom, in His goodness and love, in

24

His righteousness and holiness, *Job* 11:7–10; *Psa.* 145:3. Seen in relation to time, it is called His *eternity*. While this is usually represented in Scripture as endless duration, *Psa.* 90:2; 102:12, it really means that He is above time and therefore not subject to its limitations. For Him there is only an eternal present, and no past or future. Viewed with reference to space, it is called His *immensity*. He is everywhere present, dwells in all His creatures, filling every point of space, but is in no way bounded by space, *1 Kings* 8:27; *Psa.* 139:7–10; *Isa.* 66:1; *Jer.* 23:23, 24; *Acts* 17:27, 28.

d.   *The simplicity of God.* By ascribing simplicity to God we mean that He is not composed of various parts, such as the body and soul in man, and for that very reason is not subject to division. The three persons in the Godhead are not so many parts of which the divine essence is composed. The whole being of God belongs to each one of the Persons. Hence we can also say that God and His attributes are one, and that He is life, light, love, righteousness, truth, and so on.

2.   THE COMMUNICABLE ATTRIBUTES. These are the attributes of which we find some resemblance in man. It should be borne in mind, however, that what we see in man is only a finite (limited) and imperfect likeness of that which is infinite (unlimited) and perfect in God. Here we have:

a.   *The knowledge of God.* This is *that perfection of God whereby He, in a manner all His own, knows Himself and all things possible and actual.* God has this knowledge in Himself, and does not obtain it from without. It is always complete and always present in His mind. And because it is all-comprehensive, it is called *omniscience.* He knows all things, past, present and future, and not only the things that have real existence, but also those which are merely possible. *1 Kings* 8:29; *Psa.* 139:1–16; *Isa.* 46: 10; *Ezek.* 11:5; *Acts* 15:18; *John* 21:17; *Heb.* 4:13.

b.   *The wisdom of God.* God's wisdom is an aspect of His knowledge. It is the virtue of God which manifests itself in the selection of worthy ends and in the choice of the best means for the realization of those ends. The final end to which He makes all things subservient is His own glory. *Rom.* 11:33; *1 Cor.* 2:7; *Eph.* 1:6, 12, 14; *Col.* 1:16.

c.   *The goodness of God.* God is good, that is, perfectly holy, in Himself. But this is not the goodness we have in mind here. In this connection we refer to the divine goodness that reveals itself in doing well unto others. *It is that perfection which prompts Him to deal kindly and bounteously with all His creatures.* The Bible refers to it repeatedly, *Psa.* 36:6; 104:21; 145:8, 9, 16; *Matt.* 5:45; *Acts* 14:17.

d.   *The love of God.* This is often called the most central attribute of God, but it is doubtful whether it should be regarded as more central than the other perfections of God. *In virtue of it He delights in His own perfections and in man as the reflection of His image.* It may be considered from various points of view. The unmerited love of God which reveals itself in pardoning sin is called His *grace, Eph.* 1:6, 7; 2:7–9; *Titus* 2:11. That love relieving the misery of those who are bearing the consequences of sin is known as His *mercy* or *tender compassion, Luke* 1:54, 72, 78; *Rom.* 15:9; 9:16, 18; *Eph.* 2:4. And when it bears with the sinner who does not heed the instructions and warnings of God it is named His *longsuffering* or *forbearance, Rom.* 2:4; 9:22; *1 Pet.* 3:20; *2 Pet.* 3:15.

e.   *The holiness of God.* God's holiness is first of all *that divine perfection by which He is absolutely distinct from all His creatures, and exalted above them in infinite majesty. Exod.* 15:11; *Isa.* 57:15. But it denotes in the second place *that He is free from all moral impurity or sin, and is therefore morally perfect.* In the presence of the holy God man is deeply conscious of his sin, *Job* 34:10; *Isa.* 6:5; *Hab.* 1:13.

f.   *The righteousness of God.* The righteousness of God is *that perfection by which He maintains Himself as the Holy One over against every violation of His holiness.* In virtue of it He maintains a moral government in the world and imposes a just law on man, rewarding obedience and punishing disobedience, *Psa.* 99:4; *Isa.* 33:22; *Rom.* 1:32. The justice of God which manifests itself in the giving of rewards is called His *remunerative justice;* and that which reveals itself in meting out punishment is known as His *retributive justice.* The former is really an expression of His love, and the latter of His wrath.

g.   *The veracity of God.* This is *that perfection of God in virtue of which He is true in His inner being, in His revelation, and in His relation to His people.* He is the true God over against the idols, knows things as they really are, and is faithful in the fulfilment of His promises. From the last point of view this attribute is also called God's *faithfulness*. *Num.* 23:19; *1 Cor.* 1:9; *2 Tim.* 2:13; *Heb.* 10:23.

h.   *The sovereignty of God.* This may be considered from two different points of view, namely, *His sovereign will*, and *His sovereign power.* The will of God is represented in Scripture as the final cause of all things, *Eph.* 1:11; *Rev.* 4:11. On the basis of *Deut.* 29:29 it is customary to distinguish between the *secret* and the *revealed* will of God. *The former is the will of God's decree, which is hidden in God and can be known only from its effects, and the latter is the will of His precept, which is revealed in the law and in the gospel.* God's will respecting His creatures is absolutely free, *Job* 11:10; 33:13; *Psa.* 115:3; *Prov.* 21:1; *Matt.* 20:15; *Rom.* 9:15–18; *Rev.* 4:11. The sinful deeds of man are also under the control of His sovereign will, *Gen.* 50:20; *Acts* 2:23.

The power to execute His will is called his *omnipotence.* That God is omnipotent does not mean that He can do everything. The Bible teaches us that there are some things which God cannot do. He cannot lie, sin, deny Himself, *Num.* 23:19; *1 Sam.* 15:29; *2 Tim.* 2:13; *Heb.* 6:18; *James* 1:13, 17. It does mean *that He can, by the mere exercise of His will, bring to pass whatsoever He has decided to accomplish, and that, if He so desired, He could do even more than that*, *Gen.* 18:14; *Jer.* 32:27; *Zech.* 8:6; *Matt.* 3:9; 26:53.

To memorize. Passages to prove God's:

a. *Incommunicable attributes:*
Independence. John 5:26. 'For as the Father hath life in Himself, even so He gave to the Son also to have life in Himself.'
Immutability. Mal. 3:6. 'For I, Jehovah, change not; therefore ye, O sons of Jacob, are not consumed.' *James* 1:17. 'Every good gift and every perfect gift is from above, coming down from the Father of lights, with whom can be no variation, neither shadow that is cast by turning.'
Eternity. Psa. 90:2. 'Before the mountains were brought forth, or ever Thou hadst formed the earth and the world, even from everlasting to everlasting, Thou art God.' *Psa.* 102:27. 'But Thou art the same, and Thy years have no end.'

Omnipresence. Psa. 139:7–10. 'Whither shall I go from Thy Spirit? Or whither shall I flee from Thy presence? If I ascend up into heaven, Thou art there: if I make my bed in Sheol, behold Thou art there. If I take the wings of the morning, and dwell in the uttermost parts of the sea; even there shall Thy hand lead me, and Thy right hand shall hold me.' *Jer.* 23:23, 24. 'Am I a God at hand, saith Jehovah, and not a God afar off? Can any hide himself in secret places so that I shall not see him? saith Jehovah. Do I not fill heaven and earth? saith Jehovah.'

b. *Communicable attributes:*

Omniscience. John 21:17b. 'And he said unto Him, Lord, Thou knowest all things; Thou knowest that I love Thee.' *Heb.* 4.13. 'And there is no creature that is not manifest in His sight; but all things are naked and laid open before the eyes of Him with whom we have to do.'

Wisdom. Psa. 104:24. 'O Jehovah, how manifold are Thy works! In wisdom hast Thou made them all.' *Dan.* 2:20, 21b. 'Blessed be the name of God for ever and ever; for wisdom and might are His . . . He giveth wisdom unto the wise, and knowledge to them that have understanding.'

Goodness. Psa. 86:5. 'For Thou, Lord, art good, and ready to forgive, and abundant in loving kindness unto all them that call upon Thee.' *Psa.* 118:29. 'O give thanks unto Jehovah, for He is good; for His lovingkindness endureth for ever.'

Love. John 3:16. 'God so loved the world, that He gave His only begotten Son, that whosoever believeth in Him should not perish, but have eternal life.' *1 John* 4:8. 'He that loveth not knoweth not God; for God is love.'

Grace. Neh. 9:17b. 'But Thou art a God ready to pardon, gracious and merciful, slow to anger, and abundant in lovingkindness.' *Rom.* 3:24. 'Being justified freely by His grace through the redemption that is in Christ Jesus.'

Mercy. Rom. 9:18. 'So then He hath mercy on whom He will and whom He will He hardeneth.' *Eph.* 2:4, 5. 'But God, being rich in mercy, for His great love wherewith He loved us, even when we were dead through our trespasses, made us alive together with Christ:'

Longsuffering or forbearance. Num. 14:18. 'Jehovah is slow to anger, and abundant in lovingkindness, forgiving iniquity and transgression.' *Rom.* 2:4. 'Or despisest thou the riches of His goodness and forbearance and longsuffering, not knowing that the goodness of God leadeth thee to repentance?'

Holiness. Exod. 15:11. 'Who is like unto Thee, O Jehovah, among the gods? Who is like Thee, glorious in holiness, fearful in praises, doing wonders?' *Isa.* 6:3b. 'Holy, holy, holy, is Jehovah of hosts: the whole earth is full of His glory.'

Righteousness or justice. Psa. 89:14. 'Righteousness and justice are the foundation of Thy throne.' *Psa.* 145:17. 'Jehovah is righteous in all His ways, and gracious in all His works.' *1 Pet.* 1:17. 'And if ye call on Him as Father, who without respect of persons judgeth according to each man's work, pass the time of your sojourning in fear.'

Veracity or faithfulness. Num. 23:19. 'God is not a man, that He should lie, neither the son of man, that He should repent. Hath He said, and will He not do it? Or hath He spoken, and will He not make it good?' *2 Tim.* 2:13. 'If we are faithless, he abideth faithful; for He cannot deny Himself.'

Sovereignty. Eph. 1:11. 'In whom also we were made a heritage, having been foreordained according to the purpose of Him who worketh all things after the council of His will.' *Rev.* 4:11. 'Worthy art Thou, our Lord and our God, to receive the glory and the honour and the power; for Thou didst create all things, and because of Thy will they were, and were created.'

Secret and revealed will. Deut. 29:29. 'The secret things belong unto Jehovah our God; but the things that are revealed belong unto us and to our children for ever, that we may do all the words of this law.'

Omnipotence. Job 42:2. 'I know that Thou canst do all things.' *Matt.* 19:26. 'With God all things are possible.' *Luke* 1:37. 'For with God nothing shall be impossible' (AV).

For Further Study:

a. Give instances in which the Bible identifies God and His attributes, *Jer.* 23:6; *Heb.* 12:29; *1 John* 1:5; 4:16.

b. How can God be just and gracious to the sinner at the same time? *Zech.* 9:9; *Rom.* 3:24–26.

c. Prove from Scripture that God's foreknowledge includes conditional events. *1 Sam.* 23:10–13; *2 Kings* 13:19; *Psa.* 81: 13–15; 48:18; *Jer.* 38:17–20; *Ezek.* 3:6; *Matt.* 11:21.

Questions for Review:

1. How do we divide the attributes of God?
2. Which belong to each one of these classes?
3. What is the independence of God?
4. What is His immutability?
5. How can we explain the fact that the Bible apparently ascribes change to God?
6. What is God's eternity and immensity or omnipresence?
7. What is the simplicity of God, and how can we prove it?
8. What is the nature and extent of God's knowledge?
9. How is His wisdom related to His knowledge?
10. What is the goodness of God? Are any other names used for it?
11. Should we speak of love as more central in God than His other attributes?
12. How do we distinguish God's grace, mercy, and long suffering?
13. What is the holiness of God?
14. In what does God reveal His righteousness?
15. What is included in the veracity of God?
16. What distinction do we apply to the will of God?
17. Do the secret and the revealed will of God ever conflict?
18. Does God's omnipotence imply that He can do everything?

7

The Trinity

1.   STATEMENT OF THE DOCTRINE. The Bible teaches that, while God is one, He exists in three Persons, called Father, Son, and Holy Spirit. These are not three persons in the ordinary sense of the word; they are not three individuals, but rather modes or forms in which the Divine Being exists. At the same time they are of such a nature that they can enter into personal relations. The Father can speak to the Son and vice versa, and both can send forth the Spirit. The real mystery of the Trinity consists in this, that each one of the Persons possesses the whole of the divine essence, and that this has no existence outside of and apart from the Persons. The three are not subordinate in being the one to the other, though it may be said that in order of existence the Father is first, the Son second, and the Holy Spirit third, an order which is also reflected in their work.

2.   SCRIPTURE PROOF FOR THE TRINITY. The Old Testament contains some indications of more than one Person in God. God speaks of Himself in the plural, *Gen.* 1:26; 11:7; the Angel of Jehovah is represented as a divine Person, *Gen.* 16:7–13; 18:1–21; 19:1–22; and the Spirit is spoken of as a distinct Person, *Isa.* 48:16; 63:10. Moreover, there are some passages in which the Messiah is speaking and mentions two other Persons, *Isa.* 48:16; 61:1; 63:9,10. Due to the progress of revelation, the New Testament contains clear proofs. The strongest proof is found in the facts of redemption. The Father sends the Son into the world, and the Son sends the Holy Spirit. Moreover, there are several passages in which the three Persons are expressly mentioned, such as the great commission, *Matt.* 28:19, and the apostolic blessing, *2 Cor.* 13:14; cf. *Luke* 3:21–22; 1:35; *1 Cor.* 12:4–6; *1 Pet.* 1:2.

This doctrine was denied by the Socinians in the days of the Reformation, and is rejected also by the Unitarians and the Modernists of our own day. If they speak of the Trinity at all, they represent it as consisting of the Father, the man Jesus, and divine influence which is called the Spirit of God.

3. THE FATHER. The name 'Father' is frequently applied in Scripture to the triune God, as the creator of all things, *1 Cor.* 8:6; *Heb.* 12:9; *James* 1:17; as the Father of Israel, *Deut.* 32:6; *Isa.* 63:16; and as the Father of believers, *Matt.* 5:45; 6:6, 9, 14; *Rom.* 8:15. In a deeper sense, however, it is applied to the First Person of the Trinity, to express His relation to the Second Person, *John* 1:14, 18; 8:54; 14:12, 13. This is the original Fatherhood, of which all earthly fatherhood is but a faint reflection. *The distinctive characteristic of the Father is that He generates the Son from all eternity.* The works particularly ascribed to Him are those of planning the work of redemption, creation and providence, and representing the Trinity in the Counsel of Redemption.

4. THE SON. The second person in the Trinity is called 'Son' or 'Son of God'. He bears this name, however, not only as the only begotten of the Father, *John* 1:14, 18; 3:16, 18; *Gal.* 4:4, but also as the Messiah chosen of God, *Matt.* 8:29; 26:63; *John* 1:49; 11:27, and in virtue of His special birth through the operation of the Holy Spirit, *Luke* 1:32, 35. *His special characteristic as the Second Person of the Trinity is that He is eternally begotten of the Father,* Psa. 2:7; *Acts* 13:33; *Heb.* 1:5. *By means of eternal generation the Father is the cause of the personal existence of the Son within the Divine Being.* The works more particularly ascribed to Him are works of mediation. He mediated the work of creation, *John* 1:3, 10; *Heb.* 1:2, 3, and mediates the work of redemption, *Eph.* 1:3–14.

5. THE HOLY SPIRIT. Though Socinians, Unitarians and present-day Modernists speak of the Holy Spirit merely as a power or an influence of God, He clearly stands out in the pages of the Bible as a Person, *John* 14:16, 17, 26; 15:26; 16:7–15; *Rom* 8:26. He has intelligence, *John* 14:26, feeling, *Isa.* 63:10; *Eph.* 4:30, and will, *Acts* 16:7; *1*

Cor. 12:11. Scripture represents Him as speaking, searching, testifying, commanding, revealing, striving, and making intercession. Moreover, He is clearly distinguished from His own power in *Luke* 1:35; 4:14; *Acts* 10:38; *1 Cor.* 2:4. *His special characteristic is that He proceeds from the Father and the Son by spiration, John* 15:26; 16:7; *Rom.* 8:9; *Gal.* 4:6. In general it may be said that it is His task to bring things to completion both in creation and redemption, *Gen.* 1:3; *Job* 26:13; *Luke* 1:35; *John* 3:34; *1 Cor.* 12:4–11; *Eph.* 2:22.

To memorize. Passages to prove:

a. *The Trinity:*
Isa. 61:1. 'The Spirit of the Lord Jehovah is upon Me' (the Messiah), cf. *Luke* 4:17, 18.
Matt. 28:19. 'Go ye therefore and make disciples of all the nations, baptizing them into the name of the Father and of the Son and of the Holy Spirit.'
2 Cor. 13:14. 'The grace of the Lord Jesus Christ and the love of God, and the communion of the Holy Spirit be with you all.'

b. *Eternal generation:*
Psa. 2:7. 'I will tell of the decree, Jehovah said unto me, Thou art my Son; this day I have begotten Thee.'
John 1:14. 'And the Word became flesh, and dwelt among us (and we beheld His glory, glory as of the only begotten from the Father), full of grace and truth.'

c. *Procession of the Holy Spirit:*
John 15:26. 'But when the Comforter is come, whom I will send unto you from the Father, even the Spirit of truth, which proceedeth from the Father, He shall bear witness of Me."

For Further Study:
a.   In what sense can we speak of a general Fatherhood of God? *1 Cor.* 8:6; *Eph.* 3:14,15; *Heb.* 12:9; *James* 1:17. Cf. also *Num.* 16:22.

b. Can you prove the deity of the incarnate Son? *John* 1:1; 20:28; *Phil.* 2:6; *Titus* 2:13; *Jer.* 23:5, 6; *Isa.* 9:6; *John* 1:3; *Rev.* 1:8; *Col.* 1:17; *John* 14:1; *2 Cor.* 13:14.

c. How do the following passages prove the personality of the Holy Spirit? *Gen.* 1:2; 6:3; *Luke* 12:12; *John* 14:26; 15:26; 16:8; *Acts* 8:29; 13:2; *Rom.* 8:11; *1 Cor.* 2:10, 11.

d. What works are ascribed to the Spirit in *Psa.* 33:6; 104:30; *Exod.* 28:3; *2 Pet.* 1:21; *1 Cor.* 3:16; 12:4 ff.?

Questions for Review:

1. Can we discover the doctrine of the Trinity from nature?
2. Are there three separate individuals in God?
3. Is one Person subordinate to another in God?
4. How can we prove the Trinity from the Old Testament?
5. What is the strongest proof for the Trinity?
6. What New Testament passages best prove it?
7. In what different senses is the name 'Father' applied to God?
8. What works are more particularly ascribed to each one of the Persons?
9. In what different senses is the name 'Son' applied to Christ?
10. What is the special characteristic of each Person?
11. How do you prove that the Holy Spirit is a Person?

THE WORKS OF GOD

8

The Divine Decrees

1.　THE DIVINE DECREES IN GENERAL. The decree of God is His eternal plan or purpose, in which He has foreordained all things that come to pass. Since it includes many particulars, we often speak of the divine decrees in the plural, though in reality there is but a single decree. It covers all the works of God in creation and redemption, and also embraces the actions of men, not excluding their sinful deeds. But while it rendered the entrance of sin into the world certain, it does not make God responsible for our sinful deeds. His decree with respect to sin is a permissive decree.

a. *Characteristics of the decree.* The decree of God is founded in wisdom, *Eph.* 3:9–11, though we do not always understand it. It was formed in the depths of eternity, and is therefore *eternal* in the strictest sense of the word, *Eph.* 3:11. Moreover, it is *effectual,* so that everything that is included in it certainly comes to pass, *Isa.* 46:10. The plan of God is also *unchangeable,* because He is faithful and true, *Job* 23:13, 14; *Isa.* 46:10; *Luke* 22:22. It is *unconditional,* that is, its execution does not depend on any action of man but even renders such action certain, *Acts* 2:23; *Eph.* 2:8. Moreover, it is *all-inclusive,* embracing the good and the wicked actions of men, *Gen.* 50:20, the duration of man's life, *Job* 14:5; *Psa.* 39:4, and the place of his habitation, *Acts* 17:26. With respect to sin it is *permissive.*

b. *Objections to the doctrine of the decrees.* Many do not believe in the doctrine of the decrees, and raise especially three objections. (1) *It is inconsistent with the moral freedom of man.* But the Bible clearly teaches not only that God has decreed the free acts of man, but also that man is none the less free and responsible for his acts, *Gen.* 50:19, 20; *Acts* 2:23; 4:27–29. We may not be able to harmonize the two altogether, but it is evident from Scripture that the one does not cancel the other. (2) *It makes people slothful in seeking salvation.* They feel that, if God has determined whether they will be saved or not, it makes no difference what they may do. But this is hardly correct, because man does not know what God has decreed respecting him. Moreover, God has decreed not only the final destiny of man, but also the means by which it will be realized. And seeing that the end is decreed only as the result of the appointed means, it encourages rather than discourages their use. (3) *It makes God the author of sin.* It may be said, however, that the decree merely makes God the author of free moral beings, who are themselves the authors of sin. Sin is made certain by the decree, but God does not Himself produce it by His direct action. At the same time it must be admitted that the problem of God's relation to sin remains a mystery which we cannot fully solve.

2.   PREDESTINATION. *Predestination is the plan or purpose of God respecting His moral creatures.* It pertains to men, both good and bad, to angels and devils, and to Christ as the Mediator. Predestination includes two parts, namely, election and reprobation.

a. *Election.* The Bible speaks of election in more than one sense, as (1) the election of Israel as the Old Testament people of God, *Deut.* 4:37; 7:6–8; 10:15; *Hos.* 13:5; (2) the election of persons to some special office or service, *Deut.* 18:5; *1 Sam.* 10:24; *Psa.* 78:70; and (3) the election of individuals unto salvation, *Matt.* 22:14; *Rom.* 11:5; *Eph.* 1:4. The last is the election to which we refer in this connection. It may be defined as *God's eternal purpose to save some of the human race in and by Jesus Christ.*

b. *Reprobation.* The doctrine of election naturally implies that God did not intend to save all. If He purposed to save some, He naturally also purposed not to save others. This is also in harmony with the teachings of Scripture, *Matt.* 11:25, 26; *Rom.* 9:13, 17, 18, 21, 22; 11:7, 8; *2 Pet.* 2:9; *Jude* 4. Reprobation may be defined as *God's eternal purpose to pass some men by with the operation of His special grace, and to punish them for their sin.* It really embodies a twofold purpose therefore: (1) to pass some by in the bestowal of saving grace; and (2) to punish them for their sins.

It is sometimes said that the doctrine of predestination exposes God to the charge of injustice. But this is hardly correct. We could speak of injustice only if man had a claim on God, and God owed man eternal salvation. But the situation is entirely different if all men have forfeited the blessings of God, as they have. No one has the right to call God to account for electing some and rejecting others. He would have been perfectly just if He had not saved any, *Matt.* 20:14, 15; *Rom.* 9:14, 15.

To memorize. Passages pertaining to:

a. *God's decree in general:*
Eph. 1:11. 'In whom also we were made a heritage, having been foreordained according to the purpose of Him who worketh all things after the counsel of His will.'
Psa. 33:11. 'The counsel of Jehovah standeth fast forever, the thoughts of His heart to all generations.'
Isa. 46:10. 'Declaring the end from the beginning, and from ancient times things that are not yet done; saying, My counsel shall stand, and I will do all my pleasure.'

b. *Predestination:*
Eph. 1:11, see above under a.
Psa. 2:7. 'I will tell of the decree: Jehovah said unto me, Thou art my Son; this day have I begotten Thee.'
Eph. 1:4, 5. 'Even as He chose us in Him before the foundation of the world, that we should be holy and without blemish before Him in love, having foreordained us unto adoption as sons through Jesus Christ unto Himself, according to the good pleasure of His will.'
Rom. 11:5. 'Even so then at this present time also there is a remnant according to the election of grace.'
Rom. 9:13. 'Even as it is written, Jacob I loved, but Esau I hated.'
Rom. 9:18. 'So then He hath mercy on whom He will, and whom He will He hardeneth.'

For Further Study:

a. Is foreknowledge the same as foreordination or predestination? *Acts* 2:23; *Rom.* 8:29; 11:2; *1 Pet.* 1:2.

b. How does the Bible indicate that Christ was also an object of predestination? *Psa.* 2:7; *Isa.* 42:1; *1 Pet.* 1:20; 2:4. In what sense is this to be understood?

c. What indications have we that the angels were also objects of predestination? 1 Tim. 5:21. How should we conceive of this?

Questions for Review:

1. What is the divine decree?
2. Why do we sometimes speak of 'decrees' in the plural?
3. What are the characteristics of the decree?
4. What is the nature of God's decree respecting sin?
5. What objections are raised against the doctrine of the decrees?
6. What can be said in answer to these?
7. How is predestination related to the decree in general?
8. Who are the objects of predestination?
9. How must we conceive of the predestination of the angels and of Christ?
10. In what different sense does the Bible speak of election?
11. What does reprobation include, and what proof is there for it?
12. Does the doctrine of predestination involve injustice on the part of God? If not, why not?

9

Creation

The discussion of the decrees naturally leads on to the study of their execution, which begins with the work of creation. This is the beginning and basis of all revelation, and also the foundation of all religious life.

1.   CREATION IN GENERAL. The word creation is not always used in the same sense in the Bible. In the strict sense of the word it denotes *that work of God by which He produces the world and all that is in it, partly without the use of pre-existent materials, and partly out of material that is by its nature unfit, for the manifestation of His glory.* It is represented as a work of the triune God, *Gen.* 1:2; *Job* 26:13; 33:4; *Psa.* 33:6; *Isa.* 40:12, 13; *John* 1:3; *1 Cor.* 8:6; *Col.* 1:15–17. Over against Pantheism we must maintain that it was a free act of God. He did not need the world. *Eph.* 1:11; *Rev.* 4:11. And over against Deism, that He created the world so that it always remains dependent on Him. He must uphold it from day to day, *Acts* 17:28; *Heb.* 1:3.

a. *The time of creation.* The Bible teaches us that God created the world 'in the beginning', that is, at the beginning of all temporal things. Back of this beginning lies a timeless eternity. The first part of the work of creation mentioned in *Gen.* 1:1 was strictly creation out of nothing or without the use of pre-existent material. The expression 'creation out of nothing' is not found in the Bible, but in one of the apocryphal books, *2 Macc.* 7:28. However, the, idea is clearly taught in such passages as *Gen.* 1:1; *Psa.* 33:9; 148:5; *Rom.* 4:17; *Heb.* 11:3.

b. *The final purpose of creation.* Some find the final end or purpose of creation in the happiness of man. They say that God could not make Himself the final end, because He is sufficient unto Himself.

But it would seem to be self-evident that God does not exist for man, but man for God. The creature cannot be the final end of creation. The Bible teaches us clearly that God created the world for the manifestation of His glory. Naturally, the revelation of the glory of God is not intended as an empty show to be admired by the creature, but also aims at promoting their welfare and attuning their hearts to the praise of the Creator. *Isa.* 43:7; 60:21; 61:3; *Ezek.* 36:21, 22; 39:7; *Luke* 2:14; *Rom.* 9:17; 11:36; *1 Cor.* 15:28; *Eph.* 1:5, 6, 12, 14; 3:9, 10; *Col.* 1:16.

c. *Substitutes for the doctrine of creation.* They who reject the doctrine of creation resort to one of three theories for the explanation of the world. (1) Some say that original matter is eternal and out of it the world arose, either by mere chance, or by some higher directing force. But this is impossible, because you cannot have two eternals and therefore two infinites alongside of each other. (2) Others maintain that God and the world are essentially one, and that the world is a necessary issue (outflow) of the divine being. But this view robs God of His power of self-determination, and men of their freedom and of their moral and responsible character. It also makes God responsible for all the evil there is in the world. (3) Still others take refuge in the theory of evolution. But this is clearly a mistake, since evolution offers no explanation of the world. It already presupposes something that evolves.

2.   THE SPIRITUAL WORLD. God created not only a material but also a spiritual world, consisting of the angels.

a. *Proof for the existence of angels.* Modern liberal theology has largely discarded the belief in such spiritual beings. The Bible, however, assumes their existence throughout and ascribes to them real personality, *2 Sam.* 14:20; *Matt.* 24:36; *Jude* 6; *Rev.* 14:10. Some ascribe to them airy bodies, but this is contrary to Scripture. They are pure spiritual beings (though sometimes assuming bodily forms), *Eph.* 6:12; *Heb.* 1:14, without flesh and bone, *Luke* 24:39, and therefore invisible, *Col.* 1:16. Some of them are good, holy and elect, *Mark* 8:38; *Luke* 9:26; *2 Cor.* 11:14; *1 Tim.* 5:21; *Rev.* 14:10, and others are fallen from their original state, and therefore evil, *John* 8:44; *2 Pet.* 2:4; *Jude* 6.

b. *Classes of angels.* There are evidently different classes of angels. The Bible speaks of *cherubim*, who reveal the power, majesty, and glory of God, and guard His holiness in the garden of Eden, in tabernacle and temple, and at the descent of God to the earth. *Gen.* 3:24; *Exod.* 25:18; *2 Sam.* 22:11; *Psa.* 18:10; 80:1; 99:1; *Isa.* 37:16. Alongside of these are *seraphim*, mentioned only in *Isa.* 6:2, 3, 6. They stand as servants round about the throne of the heavenly King, sing His praises, and are ever ready to do His bidding. They serve the purpose of reconciliation and prepare men for the proper approach to God.

Two angels are mentioned by name. The first of these is *Gabriel, Dan.* 8:16; 9:21; *Luke* 1:19, 26. Evidently it was his special task to convey divine revelations to man and to interpret them. The second is *Michael, Dan.* 10:13, 21; *Jude* 9; *Rev.* 12:7. In the Epistle of Jude he is called the archangel. He is the valiant warrior fighting the battles of Jehovah against the enemies of the people of God and against the evil powers in the spirit world. Besides these the Bible mentions in general terms *principalities, powers, thrones, dominions, Eph.* 1:21; 3:10; *Col.* 1:16; 2:10; *1 Pet.* 3:22. These names point to differences of rank and dignity among the angels.

c. *Work of the angels.* The angels are represented as praising God continually, *Psa.* 103:20; *Isa.* 6; *Rev.* 5:11. Since the entrance of sin into the world they serve those who inherit salvation, *Heb.* 1:14, rejoice at the conversion of sinners, *Luke* 15:10, watch over believers, *Psa.* 34:7; 91:11, protect the little ones, *Matt.* 18:10, are present in the church, *1 Cor.* 11:10; *Eph.* 3:10; *1 Tim.* 5:21, and convey believers to the bosom of Abraham, *Luke* 16:22. They also frequently bear special revelations of God, *Dan.* 9:21–23; *Zech.* 1:12–14, communicate blessings to His people, *Psa.* 91:11, 12; *Isa.* 63:9; *Dan.* 6:22; *Acts* 5:19, and execute judgments on His enemies, *Gen.* 19:1, 13; *2 Kings* 19:35; *Matt.* 13:41.

d. *Evil angels.* Besides the good there are also evil angels, who delight in opposing God and destroying His work. They were created good, but did not retain their original position, *2 Pet.* 2:4; *Jude* 6. Their special sin is not revealed, but they probably revolted against God and aspired to divine authority, cf. *2 Thess.* 2:4, 9. Satan, who was evidently one of the princes among the angels, became the recognized head of those that fell away, *Matt.* 25:41; 9:34; *Eph.* 2:2. With superhuman power he and his hosts seek to destroy the work of God. They seek to blind and mislead even the elect, and encourage the sinner in his evil way.

3.   THE MATERIAL WORLD. In *Gen.* 1:1 we have the record of the original creation of heaven and earth. The rest of the chapter is devoted to what is often called secondary creation, the completion of the work in six days.

a. *The days of creation.* The question is frequently debated, whether the days of creation were ordinary days or not. Geologists and evolutionists speak of them as long periods of time. Now the word 'day' does not always denote a period of twenty-four hours in the Scripture, cf. *Gen.* 1:5; 2:4; *Psa.* 50:15; *Eccles.* 7:14; *Zech.* 4:10. Yet the literal interpretation of the word 'day' in the narrative of creation is favoured by the following considerations: (a) The Hebrew word *yom* (day) primarily denotes an ordinary day, and should be so understood unless the context demands another interpretation. (b) The repeated mention of morning and evening favours this interpretation. (c) It was evidently an ordinary day which Jehovah set aside and hallowed as a day of rest. (d) In *Exod.* 20:9–11, Israel is commanded to labour six days and to rest on the seventh, because Jehovah made heaven and earth in six days and rested on the seventh day. (e) The last three days were evidently ordinary days, for they were determined by the earth's relation to the sun. And if they were ordinary days, why not the others?

b. *Work of the six days.* On the first day light was created, and by the separation of light and darkness day and night were constituted. This does not conflict with the idea that sun, moon, and stars were created on the fourth day, for these are not themselves light, but light-bearers. The work of the second day was also a work of separation, the separation of the waters above from the waters below by the establishment of the firmament. On the third day the work of separation is continued in the separation of the sea and the dry land. In addition to that the vegetable kingdom of plants and trees was established. By the word of His power God caused the earth to bring forth flowerless plants, vegetables, and fruit trees, each yielding seed after their kind. The fourth day brought the creation of sun, moon, and stars, to serve a variety of purposes: to divide day and night, to serve as signs of weather conditions, to determine the succession of the seasons and of days and years, and to function as lights for the earth. The work of the fifth day consisted in the creation of birds and fishes, the inhabitants of the air and of the water. Finally, the sixth day is marked by the climax of the work of creation. The higher classes of land animals were created, and the whole work was crowned by the creation of man in the image of God. His body was formed out of the dust of the earth, while his soul was an immediate creation of God. On the seventh day God rested from His creative labours and delighted in the contemplation of His work.

Notice the parallel between the work of the first and that of the last three days:

1.	4.
The creation of light.	Creation of light-bearers.
2.	5.
Creation of expanse and separation of waters.	Creation of fowls of the air and fishes of the sea.
3.	6.
Separation of waters and dry land, and preparation of the earth as a habitation for man and beast.	Creation of the beasts of the field, the cattle, and all creeping things; and man.

c. *The theory of evolution.* Evolutionists want to substitute their view of the origin of things for the scriptural doctrine. They believe that from the simplest forms of matter and life all existing species of plants and animals (including man), and also the various manifestations of life, such as intelligence, morality, and religion, developed by a perfectly natural process, purely as the result of natural forces. This is merely an assumption, however, and one that fails at several points. Moreover, it is in hopeless conflict with the narrative of creation as it is found in the Bible.

To memorize. Passages bearing on:

a. *The fact of creation:*
Gen. 1:1. 'In the beginning God created the heavens and the earth.'

Psa. 33:6. 'By the word of Jehovah were the heavens made, and all the host of them by the breath of His mouth.'

John 1:3. 'All things were made through Him; and without Him was not anything made that hath been made.'

Heb. 11:3. 'By faith we understand that the worlds have been framed by the word of God, so that what is seen hath not been made out of things which appear.'

b. *The final end of creation:*

Isa. 43:6, 7. 'Bring . . . every one that is called by my name, and whom I have created for my glory, whom I have formed; yea, whom I have made.'

Psa. 19:1. 'The heavens declare the glory of God; and the firmament showeth His handiwork.'

Psa. 148:13. 'Let them praise the name of Jehovah; for His name alone is exalted: His glory is above the earth and the heavens.' See also the context.

c. *Angels:*

Psa. 103:20. 'Bless Jehovah, ye His angels, that are mighty in strength, that fulfil His word, hearkening unto the voice of His word.'

Heb. 1:14. 'Are they not all ministering spirits, sent forth to do service for the sake of them that shall inherit salvation?'

Jude 6. 'And angels that kept not their principality, but left their proper habitation, He hath kept in everlasting bonds under darkness unto the judgment of the great day.'

d. *Time of creation:*

Gen. 1:1. 'In the beginning God created the heavens and the earth.'

Exod. 20:11. 'For in six days Jehovah made heaven and earth, the sea, and all that in them is, and rested the seventh day: wherefore Jehovah blessed the sabbath day and hallowed it.'

For Further Study:

a.   In what sense is the word 'to create' used in *Psa.* 51:10; 104:30; *Isa.* 45:7?

b.   Do *Gen.* 1:11, 12, 20, 24 favour the idea of evolution? Cf. *Gen.* 1:21, 25; 2:9.

c.   Do the following passages tell us anything about the sin of the angels? If so, what? *2 Pet.* 2:4; *Jude* 6; cf. also *2 Thess.* 2:4–12.

Questions for Review:

1.   What is creation?
2.   Was creation a free or a necessary act of God?
3.   Is the word 'create' always used in the same sense in Scripture?
4.   Does the Bible prove creation out of nothing? Where?
5.   What two views are there as to the final end of creation?
6.   In what sense is the glory of God the final end?
7.   What substitutes have been suggested for the doctrine of creation?
8.   What is the nature of the angels?
9.   What orders of angels are named in Scripture?
10. What is the function of Gabriel and Michael?
11. What is the work of the angels?
12. What proof have we for the existence of evil angels?
13. Were they created evil?
14. Were the days in Genesis ordinary days or long periods?
15. What did God create on each of the six days?
16. Is the theory of evolution consistent with the doctrine of creation?
17. Can you name some of the points on which they differ?

10

Providence

Since God not only created the world but also upholds it, we naturally pass from the doctrine of creation to that of divine providence. This may be defined as *that work of God in which He preserves all His creatures, is active in all that happens in the world, and directs all things to their appointed end.* It includes three elements, of which the first pertains primarily to the *being*, the second to the *activity*, and the third to the *purpose* of all things.

1. THE ELEMENTS OF DIVINE PROVIDENCE. We distinguish three elements.

a. *Divine preservation.* This is *that continuous work of God by which He upholds all things.* While the world has a distinct existence and is not a part of God, it nevertheless has the ground of its continued existence in God and not in itself. It endures through a continued exercise of divine power by which all things are maintained in being and action. This doctrine is taught in the following passages: *Psa.* 136:25; 145:15; *Neh.* 9:6; *Acts* 17:28; *Col.* 1:17; *Heb.* 1:3.

b. *Divine concurrence.* This may be defined as *that work of God by which He co-operates with all His creatures and causes them to act precisely as they do.* It implies that there are real secondary causes in the world, such as the powers of nature and the will of man, and asserts that these do not work independently of God. God works in every act of His creatures, not only in their good but also in their evil acts. He stimulates them to action, accompanies their action at every moment, and makes this action effective. However, we should never think of God and man as equal causes; the former is the primary, and the latter only a secondary cause. Neither should we conceive of them as each doing a part of the work like a team of horses. The same deed is in its entirety both a deed of God and a deed of man. Moreover, we should guard against the idea that this co-operation makes God responsible for man's sinful deeds. This doctrine is based on Scripture, *Deut.* 8:18; *Psa.* 104:20, 21, 30; *Amos* 3:6; *Matt.* 5:45; 10:29; 14:17; *Phil.* 2:13.

c. *Divine government.* This is *the continued activity of God whereby He rules all things so that they answer to the purpose of their existence.* God is represented as King of the universe both in the Old and in the New Testament. He adapts His rule to the nature of the creatures which He governs; His government of the physical world differs from that of the spiritual world. It is universal, *Psa.* 103:19; *Dan.* 4:34, 35, includes the most insignificant things, *Matt.* 10:29–31, and that which is seemingly accidental, *Prov.* 16:33, and bears on both the good and the evil deeds of man, *Phil.* 2:13; *Gen.* 50:20; *Acts* 14:16.

2. MISCONCEPTIONS OF DIVINE PROVIDENCE. In the doctrine of providence we should guard against two misconceptions:

a. *The Deistic conception.* This is to the effect that God's concern with the world is of the most general nature. He created the world, established its laws, set it in motion, and then withdrew from it. He wound it up like a clock, and now lets it run off. It is only when something goes wrong that He interferes with its regular operation. God is only a God afar off.

b. *The Pantheistic conception.* Pantheism does not recognize the distinction between God and the world. It identifies the two, and therefore leaves no room for providence in the proper sense of the word. There are, strictly speaking, no such things as secondary causes. God is the direct author of all that transpires in the world. Even the acts which we ascribe to man are really acts of God. God is only a God that is near, and not a God afar off.

3. EXTRAORDINARY PROVIDENCES OR MIRACLES. We distinguish between general and special providences, and among the latter the miracles occupy an important place. A miracle is a supernatural work of God, that is a work which is accomplished without the mediation of secondary causes. If God sometimes apparently uses

secondary causes in the production of miracles, He employs them in an unusual way, so that the work is after all supernatural. Some regard miracles as impossible, because they involve a violation of the laws of nature. But this is a mistake. The so-called laws of nature merely represent God's usual method of working. And the fact that God generally works according to a definite order does not mean that He cannot depart from this order, and cannot without violating or disturbing it bring about unusual results. Even man can lift up his hand and throw a ball into the air in spite of the law of gravitation and without in any way disturbing its operation. Surely, this is not impossible for the omnipotent God. The miracles of the Bible are means of revelation. *Num.* 16:28; *Jer.* 32:20; *John* 2:11; 5:36.

To memorize. Passages referring to:

a. *Preservation:*

Psa. 36:6b. 'O Jehovah, thou preservest man and beast.'

Neh. 9:6. 'Thou art Jehovah, even thou alone; thou hast made heaven, the heaven of heavens, with all their host, the earth and all things that are thereon, the seas and all that is in them, and thou preservest them all.'

Col. 1:17. 'And He is before all things, and in Him all things consist.'

b. *Concurrence:*

Deut. 8:18a. 'But thou shalt remember Jehovah thy God, for it is He that giveth thee power to get wealth.'

Amos 3:6. 'Shall the trumpet be blown in a city, and the people not be afraid? shall evil befall a city, and Jehovah hath not done it?'

Phil. 2:13. 'For it is God who worketh in you both to will and to work, for His good pleasure.'

c. *Government:*

Psa. 103:19. 'Jehovah hath established His throne in the heavens; and His Kingdom ruleth over all.'

Dan. 4:3b. 'His kingdom is an everlasting kingdom, and His dominion is from generation to generation.'

1 Tim. 6:15. 'Which in its own times He shall show, who is the blessed and only Potentate, the King of kings, and Lord of lords.'

d. *Miracles and their design:*

Exod. 15:11. 'Who is like unto Thee, O Jehovah, among the gods? Who is like Thee glorious in holiness, fearful in praises, doing wonders?'

Psa. 72:18. 'Blessed be Jehovah God, the God of Israel, who only doeth wondrous things.'

Mark 2:10, 11. 'But that ye may know that the Son of man hath authority on earth to forgive sins, He saith to the sick of the palsy, I say unto thee, Arise, take up thy bed, and go unto thy house.'

John 2:11. 'This beginning of miracles did Jesus in Cana of Galilee, and manifested His glory; and His disciples believed on Him.'

For Further Study:

a. Name some examples of special providences. Cf. *Deut.* 2:7; *1 Kings* 17:6, 16; *2 Kings* 4:6; *Matt.* 14:20.

b. How should belief in divine providence affect our cares? *Isa.* 41:10; *Matt.* 6:32; *Luke* 12:7; *Phil.* 4:6,7; *1 Pet.* 5:7.

c. Name some of the blessings of providence. Cf. *Isa.* 25:4; *Psa.* 121:4; *Luke* 12:7; *Deut.* 33:27; *Psa.* 37:28; *2 Tim.* 4:18.

Questions for Review:

1. How is the doctrine of providence related to that of creation?
2. What is divine providence?
3. What is the difference between general and special providence?
4. What are the objects of divine providence?
5. What are the three elements of providence, and how do they differ?
6. How must we conceive of the divine concurrence?
7. How far does the divine government extend?
8. What is a miracle, and what purpose do the scriptural miracles serve?
9. Why do some consider miracles impossible?

THE DOCTRINE OF MAN IN RELATION TO GOD

I I

Man in His Original State

From the discussion of the doctrine of God we pass on to that of man, the crown of God's handiwork.

1.   THE ESSENTIAL ELEMENTS OF HUMAN NATURE. The usual view is that man consists of two parts, body and soul. This is in harmony with the self-consciousness of man, and is also borne out by a study of Scripture, which speaks of man as consisting of 'body and soul', *Matt.* 6:25; 10:28, or of 'body and spirit', *Eccles.* 12:7; *1 Cor.* 5:3, 5. Some are of the opinion that the words 'soul' and 'spirit' denote different elements, and that therefore man consists of three parts, body, soul, and spirit, cf. *1 Thess.* 5:23. It is evident, however, that the two words 'soul' and 'spirit' are used interchangeably. Death is sometimes described as a giving up of the soul, *Gen.* 35:18; *1 Kings* 17:21, and sometimes as the giving up of the spirit, *Luke* 23:46; *Acts* 7:59. The dead are in some cases named 'souls', *Rev.* 6:9; 20:4, and in others 'spirits', *1 Pet.* 3:19; *Heb.* 12:23. The two terms denote the spiritual element in man from different points of view. As spirit it is the principle of life and action, which controls the body, and as soul it is the personal subject, which thinks and feels and wills, and in some cases the seat of the affections.

2.   THE ORIGIN OF THE SOUL IN EACH INDIVIDUAL. There are three views respecting the origin of the individual souls.

a. *Pre-existentialism.* Some advocated the idea that the souls of men existed in a previous state, and that something that happened then accounts for their present condition. A few found in this an explanation of the fact that man is born as a sinner. This view finds no favour now.

b. *Traducianism.* According to this view men derive their souls as well as their bodies from their parents. This is the common view in the Lutheran Church. Support for it is found in the fact that nothing is said about the creation of Eve's soul, and that descendants are said to be in the loins of their Fathers, *Gen* 46:26; *Heb.* 7:9, 10. Furthermore, it seems to be favoured by the fact that in the case of animals both body and soul are passed on from the old to the young, by the inheritance of family traits and peculiarities, and by the inheritance of sinful corruption, which is a matter of the soul more than of the body. However, it is burdened with serious difficulties. It either makes the parents creators, or assumes that the soul of man can be divided into various parts. Moreover, it endangers the sinlessness of Jesus.

c. *Creationism.* This holds that each soul is a direct creation of God, of which the time cannot be precisely determined. The soul is supposed to be created pure, but to become sinful even before birth by entering into that complex of sin by which humanity as a whole is burdened. This view is common in Reformed circles. It is favoured by the fact that Scripture represents the body and the soul of man as having different origins, *Eccles.* 12:7; *Isa.* 42:5; *Zech.* 12:1; *Heb.* 12:9. Moreover, it is more in harmony with the spiritual nature of the soul, and safeguards the sinlessness of Jesus. It is not free from difficulties, however. It does not explain the inheritance of family traits, and may seem to make God the Creator of sinful souls.

3.   MAN AS THE IMAGE OF GOD. The Bible teaches that man is created in the image of God. According to *Gen.* 1:26, God said, 'Let us make man in our image, after our likeness.' The two words 'Image' and 'likeness' evidently denote the same thing. The following passages show that they are used interchangeably: *Gen.* 1:26, 27; 5:1; 9:6; *1 Cor.* 11:7; *Col.* 3:10; *James* 3:9. The word 'likeness' probably stresses the fact that the image is most like or very similar. There are different views of the image of God in man:

a. *The Roman Catholic view.* Roman Catholics find the image of God in certain natural gifts with which man is endowed, such as the spirituality of the soul, the freedom of the will, and immortality. To these God added a supernatural gift, called original righteousness, to keep the lower nature in check. This is supposed to constitute man's likeness to God.

b. *The Lutheran view.* The Lutherans are not all agreed on this point, but the prevailing opinion is that the image of God consists only in those spiritual qualities with which man was endowed at creation, namely, true knowledge, righteousness, and holiness. These may be designated original righteousness. This view is too restricted.

c. *The Reformed view.* The Reformed distinguish between the natural and the moral image of God. The former is the broader of the two, and is generally said to consist in man's spiritual, rational, moral, and immortal being. This was obscured but not lost by sin. The latter is the image of God in the more restricted sense, and consists in true knowledge, righteousness, and holiness. This was lost by sin and is restored in Christ, *Eph.* 4:24; *Col.* 3:10. Since man retained the image in the broader sense, he can still be called the image or image-bearer of God, *Gen.* 9:6; *1 Cor.* 11:7; 15:49; *James* 3:9.

4.   MAN IN THE COVENANT OF WORKS. God at once entered into covenant relationship with man. This original covenant is called the covenant of works.

a. *Scripture proof for the covenant of works.* (1) Paul draws a parallel between Adam and Christ in *Rom.* 5:12–21. In Adam all men died, but in Christ all those who are His are made alive. This means that Adam was the representative head of all men, just as Christ is now the representative head of all those who are His. (2) In *Hos.* 6:7 we read: 'But they like Adam have transgressed the covenant' (ASV). Adam's sin is called a transgression of the covenant.

b. *The elements of the covenant of works.* (1) *The parties.* A covenant is always a compact between two parties. In this case they are the triune God, the sovereign Lord of the universe, and Adam as the representative of the human race. Since these parties are very unequal, the covenant naturally partakes of the nature of an arrangement imposed

on man. (2) *The promise.* The promise of the covenant was the promise
of life in the highest sense, life raised above the possibility of death.
This is what believers now receive through Christ, the last Adam.
(3) *The condition.* The condition was that of absolute obedience. The
positive command not to eat of the tree of the knowledge of good and
evil was clearly a test of pure obedience. (4) *The penalty.* The penalty
was death in the most inclusive sense of the word, physical, spiritual,
and eternal. This consists not only in the separation of body and soul,
but more fundamentally in the separation of the soul from God.
(5) *The sacrament(s).* In all probability the tree of life was the only sacrament of this covenant – if it was indeed a sacrament. It seems to have
been appointed as a symbol and seal of life.

c. *The present validity of the covenant of works.* Arminians hold that
this covenant was wholly set aside. But this is not correct. The demand
of perfect obedience still stands for those who do not accept the righteousness of Christ. *Lev.* 18:5; *Gal.* 3:12. Though they cannot meet
the requirement, the condition stands. It holds no more, however,
for those who are in Christ, since He met the demands of the law
for them. It ceased to be a way of life, for as such it is powerless after
the Fall.

To memorize. Passages bearing on:

a. *The elements of human nature:*
Matt. 10:28. 'And be not afraid of them that kill the body, but are
not able to kill the soul: but rather fear him who is able to destroy both
soul and body in hell.'
Rom. 8:10. 'And if Christ is in you, the body is dead because of sin;
but the spirit is life because of righteousness.'

b. *The creation of the soul:*
Eccles. 12:7. 'And the dust returneth to the earth as it was, and the
spirit returneth unto God who gave it.'
Heb. 12:9. 'Furthermore, we had the fathers of our flesh to chasten us,
and we gave them reverence: shall we not much rather be in subjection
unto the Father of spirits, and live?'

c. *Man's creation in the image of God:*

Gen. 1:27. 'And God created man in His own image, in the image of God created He him; male and female created He them.'

Gen. 9:6. 'Whoso sheddeth man's blood, by man shall his blood be shed; for in the image of God made He man.'

d. *Man in general even now the image of God:*

Gen. 9:6. See above under c.

James 3:9. 'Therewith bless we the Lord and Father; and therewith curse we men, who are made in the likeness of God.'

e. *The restoration of the image of God in man:*

Eph. 4:24. 'And put on the new man, that after God hath been created in righteousness and holiness of truth.'

Col. 3:10. 'And have put on the new man, that is being renewed unto knowledge after the image of Him that created him.'

f. *The covenant of works:*

Hos. 6:7. 'But they like Adam have transgressed the covenant.'

1 Cor. 15:22. 'For as in Adam all die, so also in Christ shall all be made alive.'

For Further Study:

a. How would you explain the passages which seem to imply that man consists of three elements, *1 Thess.* 5:23; *Heb.* 4:12; compare *Matt.* 22:37.

b. Does man's dominion over the rest of creation also form part of the image of God? *Gen.* 1:26, 28; *Psa.* 8:6–8; *Heb.* 2:5–9.

c. What indications of a covenant can you find in *Gen.* 2 and 3?

Questions for Review:

1. What is the usual view of the elements of human nature, and how can this be proved?

2. What other view is there, and what passages seem to support it?

3. What different views are there as to the origin of the soul?

4. What are the arguments for, and the objection to each one of these?

5. Do the words 'image' and 'likeness' denote different things?

6. What are the Roman Catholic, the Lutheran, and the Reformed views of the image of God in man?

7. What distinction do the Reformed make, and why is it important?

8. What Bible proof have we for the covenant of works?

9. Who are the parties in the covenant?

10. What are the promise, the condition, the penalty, and the sacrament of the covenant?

11. In what sense does this covenant still hold?

12. In what sense is it abolished?

I 2

Man in the State of Sin

1.   THE ORIGIN OF SIN. The Bible teaches us that sin entered the world as the result of the transgression of Adam and Eve in paradise. The first sin was occasioned by the temptation of Satan in the form of a serpent, who sowed in man's heart the seeds of distrust and unbelief. Scripture clearly indicates that the serpent, who appears as the tempter in the story of the Fall, was but an instrument of Satan, *John* 8:44; *Rom.* 16:20; *2 Cor.* 11:3; *Rev.* 12:9. The first sin consisted in man's eating of the tree of the knowledge of good and evil. This eating was sinful simply because God had forbidden it. It clearly showed that man was not willing to subject his will unconditionally to the will of God, and comprised several elements. In the intellect it revealed itself as unbelief and pride, in the will as the desire to be like God, and in the affections as an unholy satisfaction in eating of the forbidden fruit. As a result of it man lost the image of God in the restricted sense, became guilty and utterly corrupt, and fell under the sway of death, *Gen.* 3:19; *Rom.* 5:12; 6:23.

2.   THE ESSENTIAL NATURE OF SIN. At present many substitute the word 'evil' for 'sin,' but this is a poor substitute, for the word 'sin' is far more specific. It denotes a definite kind of evil, namely, a moral evil for which man is responsible and which brings him under a sentence of condemnation. The modern tendency to regard it merely as a wrong done to one's fellow beings misses the point entirely, for such a wrong can be called sin only in so far as it is contrary to the will of God. Sin is correctly defined by Scripture as 'lawlessness', *1 John* 3:4. It is lack of conformity to the law of God, and as such the opposite of that love which is required by the divine law. The Bible always contemplates it in relation to the law, *Rom.* 1:32; 2:12–14;

4:15; 5:13; *James* 2:9, 10; *1 John* 3:4. It is first of all *guilt*, making men liable to punishment, *Rom.* 3:19; 5:18; *Eph.* 2:3, and then also *inherent corruption* or moral pollution. All men are guilty in Adam, and are therefore born with a corrupt nature. *Job* 14:4; *Jer.* 17:9; *Isa.* 6:5; *Rom.* 8:5–8; *Eph.* 4:17–19. Sin has its seat in the heart of man, and from this centre influences the intellect, the will, and the affections, in fact the whole man, and finds expression through the body. *Prov.* 4:23; *Jer.* 17:9; *Matt.* 15:19, 20; *Luke* 6:45; *Heb.* 3:12. In distinction from the Roman Catholics we maintain that it does not consist in outward acts only, but includes evil thoughts, affections, and intents of the heart. *Matt.* 5:22, 28; *Rom.* 7:7; *Gal.* 5:17, 24.

3.   SIN IN THE LIFE OF THE HUMAN RACE. Three points deserve consideration here.

a. *The connection between Adam's sin and that of his descendants.* This has been explained in three different ways. (1) *The earliest explanation is called the realistic theory*, which is to the effect that God originally created one general human nature, which in course of time divided into as many parts as there are human individuals. Adam possessed the whole of this general human nature; and through his sin it became guilty and polluted. Naturally, every individual part of it shares this guilt and pollution. (2) *In the days of the Reformation the representative theory came to the foreground.* According to this view Adam stood in a twofold relation to his descendants: he was their natural head, and he was their representative as the head of the covenant. When he sinned as their representative, this sin was also imputed to them and as a result they are all born in a corrupt state. This is our Reformed view. (3) *A third theory not so well known, is that of mediate imputation.* It holds that the guilt of Adam's sin is not directly placed to our account. His corruption is passed on to his descendants, and this makes them personally guilty. They are not corrupt because they are guilty in Adam, but guilty because they are corrupt.

b. *Original and Actual Sin.* We distinguish between original and actual sin. All men are born in a sinful state and condition, which is called original sin, and is the root of all the actual sins that are committed. (1) *Original sin.* This includes both *guilt* and *pollution.* The guilt of

Adam's sin is imputed to us. Because he sinned as our representative, we are guilty in him. Moreover we also inherit his pollution, and now have a positive disposition toward sin. Man is by nature *totally depraved*. This does not mean that every man is as bad as he can be, but that sin has corrupted every part of his nature and rendered him unable to do any spiritual good. He may still do many praiseworthy things in relation to his fellow-beings, but even his best works are *radically defective*, because they are not prompted by love to God nor done in obedience to God. This total depravity and inability is denied by Pelagians, Arminians, and Modernists, but is clearly taught in Scripture *Jer.* 17:9; *John* 5:42; 6:44; 15:4, 5; *Rom.* 7:18, 23, 24; 8:7, 8; *1 Cor.* 2:14; *2 Cor.* 7:1; *Eph.* 2:1–3; 4:18; *2 Tim.* 3:2–4; *Titus* 1:15; *Heb.* 11:6. (2) *Actual sin.* The term 'actual sin' denotes not only sins consisting in outward acts, but also those conscious thoughts, desires, and decisions that proceed from original sin. They are the sins which the individual performs in distinction from his inherited nature and inclination. While original sin is one, actual sins are manifold. They may be sins of the inner life, such as pride, envy, hatred, sensual lusts, and evil desires; or sins of the outer life, such as deceit, theft, murder, adultery, and so on. Among these there is one unpardonable sin, namely, *the sin of blasphemy against the Holy Spirit*, after which a change of heart is impossible, and for which it is not necessary to pray, *Matt.* 12:31,32; *Mark* 3:28–30; *Luke* 12:10; *Heb.* 6:4–6; 10:26,27; *1 John* 5:16.

c. *The Universality of Sin.* Scripture and experience both teach us that sin is universal. Even the Pelagians do not deny this, though they ascribe it to external conditions, such as a bad environment, evil examples, and a wrong kind of education. There are passages in which the Bible directly asserts the universality of sin, such as *1 Kings* 8:46; *Psa.* 143:2; *Prov.* 20:9; *Eccles.* 7:20; *Rom.* 3:1–12, 19, 23; *Gal.* 3:22; *James* 3:2; *1 John* 1:8, 10. Moreover, it teaches that man is sinful from birth, so that this cannot be considered as the result of imitation, *Job* 14:4; *Psa.* 51:5; *John* 3:6. Even infants are considered sinful, for they are subject to death, which is the penalty for sin, *Rom.* 5:12–14. All men are by nature under condemnation, and therefore need the redemption which is in Christ Jesus. Children are never made an exception to this rule. *John* 3:3, 5; *Eph.* 2:3; *1 John* 5:12.

To memorize. Passages to prove:

a. *That sin is guilt:*

Rom. 5:18. 'So then as through one trespass the judgment came unto all men to condemnation; even so through one act of righteousness the free gift came unto all men to justification of life.'

1 John 3:4. 'Every one that doeth sin doeth also lawlessness; and sin is lawlessness.'

Eph. 2:3. 'Among whom we also all once lived in the lusts of our flesh, doing the desires of the flesh and of the mind, and were by nature children of wrath, even as the rest.'

b. *That sin is pollution:*

Jer. 17:9. 'The heart is deceitful above all things, and it is exceedingly corrupt: who can know it?'

Rom. 7:18. 'For I know that in me, that is in my flesh, dwelleth no good thing; for to will is present with me, but to do that which is good is not.'

Rom. 8:5. 'For they that are after the flesh mind the things of the flesh; but they that are after the Spirit the things of the Spirit.'

c. *That sin has its seat in the heart:*

Jer. 17:9. See above under b.

Matt. 15:19. 'For out of the heart come forth evil thoughts, murders, adulteries, fornications, thefts, false witness, railings.'

Heb. 3:12. 'Take heed, brethren, lest haply there shall be in any one of you an evil heart of unbelief, in falling away from the living God.'

d. *That Adam's guilt is imputed to us:*

Rom. 5:12. 'Through one man sin entered into the world, and death through sin; and so death passed unto all men, for that all sinned.' Also verse 19. 'For as through one man's disobedience the many were made sinners, even so through the obedience of the one shall the many be made righteous.'

1 Cor. 15:21, 22. 'For since by man came death, by man came also the resurrection of the dead. For as in Adam all die, so also in Christ shall all be made alive.'

e. *That man is totally depraved:*
Jer. 17:9; *Rom.* 7:18; 8:5. See under b. above.

f. *That sin is universal:*
1 Kings 8:46. 'For there is no man that sinneth not.'
Psa. 143:2. 'And enter not into judgment with thy servant; for in thy sight no man living is righteous.'
Rom. 3:12. 'They have all turned aside, they are together become unprofitable; there is none that doeth good, no, not so much as one.'
1 John 1:8. 'If we say that we have no sin, we deceive ourselves and the truth is not in us.'

For Further Study:
a. Can you give some other scriptural names for sin? *Job* 15:5; 33:9; *Psa.* 32:1, 2; 55:15; *Rom.* 1:18; 5:15; *1 John* 3:4.
b. Does the word 'evil' ever mean anything else than sin in Scripture? If so, what? Cf. *Exod.* 5:19; *2 Kings* 6:33; 22:16; *Psa.* 41:8; 91:10; *Prov.* 16:4.
c. Does the Bible explicitly teach that man is a sinner from birth? *Psa.* 51:5; *Isa.* 48:8.

Questions for Review:
1. What is the biblical view of the origin of sin?
2. What was the first sin, and what elements can be distinguished in it?
3. How would you prove that Satan was the real tempter?
4. What were the results of the first sin?
5. Do the words 'sin' and 'evil' mean the same thing?
6. Where does sin have its seat in man?
7. Does sin consist only in outward acts?
8. What different views are there respecting the connection between Adam's sin and that of his descendants?
9. What is original sin, and how does actual sin differ from it?
10. How do you conceive of total depravity?
11. What proof is there for the universality of sin?

13

Man in the Covenant of Grace

For the sake of clearness we distinguish between the covenant of redemption and the covenant of grace. The two are so closely related that they can be and sometimes are, considered as one. The former is the eternal foundation of the latter.

1.   THE COVENANT OF REDEMPTION. This is also called 'the counsel of peace', a name derived from *Zech.* 6:13. It is a covenant between the Father, representing the Trinity, and the Son as the representative of the elect.

a. *The scriptural basis for it.* It is clear that the plan of redemption was included in God's eternal decree, *Eph.* 1:4 ff.; 3:11; *2 Tim.* 1:9. Christ speaks of promises made to Him before He came into the world, and repeatedly refers to a commission which He received from the Father, *John* 5:30, 43; 6:38–40; 17:4–12. He is evidently a covenant head, *Rom.* 5:12–21; *1 Cor.* 15:22. In *Psa.* 2:7–9 the parties of the covenant are mentioned and a promise is indicated, and in *Psa.* 40:7, 8 the Messiah expresses His readiness to do the Father's will in becoming a sacrifice for sin.

b. *The Son in the covenant of redemption.* Christ is not only the Head but also the Surety of the covenant of redemption, *Heb.* 7:22. A surety is one who takes upon himself the legal obligations of another. Christ took the place of the sinner, to bear the penalty of sin and to meet the demands of the law for His people. By so doing He became the last Adam, a life-giving spirit, *1 Cor.* 15:45. For Christ this covenant was a covenant of works, in which He met the requirements of the original covenant, but for us it is the eternal foundation of the covenant of grace. Its benefits are limited to the elect. They only obtain the redemption and inherit the glory which Christ merited for sinners.

c. *Requirements and promises in the covenant of redemption.*

(1) The Father *required* of the Son that He should assume human nature with its present infirmities, though without sin, *Gal.* 4:4, 5; *Heb.* 2:10, 11, 14, 15; 4:15; that He should place Himself under the law to pay the penalty and to merit eternal life for the elect, *Psa.* 40:8; *John* 10:11; *Gal.* 1:4; 4:4, 5; and that He should apply His merits to His people by the renewing operation of the Holy Spirit, thus securing the consecration of their lives to God, *John* 10:28; 17:19–22; *Heb.* 5:7–9. (2) And the Father *promised* the Son that He would prepare for Him a body, *Heb.* 10:5, would anoint Him with the Holy Spirit, *Isa.* 42:1; 61:1; *John* 3:34, would support Him in His work, *Isa.* 42:6, 7; *Luke* 22:43, would deliver Him from the power of death and place Him at His own right hand, *Psa.* 16:8–11; *Phil.* 2:9–11, would enable Him to send the Spirit for the formation of the church, *John* 14:26; 15:26; 16:13, 14, would draw and preserve the elect, *John* 6:37, 39; 40, 44, 45, and would grant Him a numerous seed, *Psa.* 22:27; 72:17.

2.   THE COVENANT OF GRACE. On the basis of the covenant of redemption God established the covenant of grace. Several particulars call for consideration here.

a. *The contracting parties.* God is the first party in the covenant. He establishes the covenant and determines the relation in which the second party will stand to Him. It is not so easy to determine who the second party is. The prevailing opinion in Reformed circles is that it is the elect sinner in Christ. We should bear in mind, however, that the covenant may be viewed in two different ways: (1) *As an end in itself,* a covenant of mutual friendship or communion of life, which is realized in the course of history through the operation of the Holy Spirit. It represents a condition in which privileges are improved for spiritual ends, the promises of God are embraced by a living faith, and the promised blessings are fully realized. So conceived, it may be defined as *that gracious agreement between God and the elect sinner in Christ, in which God gives Himself with all the blessings of salvation to the elect sinner, and the latter embraces God and all His gracious gifts by faith. Deut.* 7:9; *2 Chron.* 6:14; *Psa.* 25:10, 14; 103:17, 18. (2) *As a means to an end,* a purely legal arrangement for the realization of a spiritual end. It is evident that the Bible sometimes speaks of the covenant as including some in whom the promises are never realized, such as Ishmael, Esau, the wicked sons of Eli, and the rebellious Israelites who died in their sins. The covenant may be regarded *as a purely legal agreement, in which God guarantees the blessings of salvation to all who believe.* If we think of the covenant in this broader sense, we can say that God established it with believers and their children, *Gen.* 17:7; *Acts* 2:39; *Rom.* 9:1–4.

b. *The promises and requirements of the covenant.* Every covenant has two sides; it offers certain privileges and imposes certain obligations.

i. *The promises of the covenant.* The main promise of the covenant, which includes all others, is contained in the oft-repeated words, 'I will be a God unto thee and to thy seed after thee', *Jer.* 31:33; 32:38–40; *Ezek.* 34:23–25, 30, 31; 36:25–28; *Heb.* 8:10; *2 Cor.* 6:16–18. This promise includes all others, such as the promise of temporal blessings, of justification, of the Spirit of God, and of final glorification in a life that never ends. *Job* 19:25–27; *Psa.* 16:11; 73:24–26; *Isa.* 43:25; *Jer.* 31:33, 34; *Ezek.* 36:27; *Dan.* 12:2, 3; *Gal.* 4:4, 5, 6; *Titus* 3:7; *Heb.* 11:7; *James* 2:5.

ii. *The requirements of the covenant.* The covenant of grace is not a covenant of works; it requires no work with a view to merit. However, it does contain requirements and imposes obligations on man. By meeting the demands of the covenant man earns nothing, but merely puts himself in the way in which God will communicate to him the promised blessings. Moreover, it should be borne in mind that even the requirements are covered by the promises: God gives man all that He requires of him. The two things which He demands of those who stand in covenant relationship to Him are (a) *that they accept the covenant and the covenant promises by faith, and thus enter upon the life of the covenant;* and (b) *that from the principle of the new life born within them, they con-secrate themselves to God in new obedience.*

c. *The characteristics of the covenant.* The covenant of grace is a *gra-cious* covenant, because it is a fruit and manifestation of the grace of God to sinners. It is grace from start to finish. It is also an *eternal* and inviolable covenant, to which God will always be true, though men may break it. Even in its widest extent it includes only a part of mankind, and is therefore *particular*. If its New Testament dispensation is called universal this is done only in view of the fact that it is not limited to the Jew, as the Old Testament dispensation was. This covenant is also characterized by *unity*. It is essentially the same in all dispensations, though the form of its administration changes. The essential promise is the same, *Gen.* 17:7; *Heb.* 8:10, the gospel is the same, *Gal.* 3:8, the requirement of faith is the same, *Gal.* 3:6, 7, and the Mediator is the same, *Heb.* 13:8. The Covenant is both *conditional* and *unconditional*.

It is conditional because it is dependent on the merits of Christ and because the enjoyment of the life it offers depends on the exercise of faith. But it is unconditional in the sense that it does not depend on any merits of man. And, finally, it is testamentary as a free and sovereign disposition on the part of God. It is called a 'testament' in *Heb.* 9:16, 17. This name stresses the facts, (1) *that it is a free arrangement of God;* (2) *that its New Testament dispensation was ushered in by the death of Christ;* and (3) *that in it God gives what He demands.* The covenant of grace differs from the covenant of works in that it has a *mediator.* Christ is represented as the Mediator of the new covenant, *1 Tim.* 2:5; *Heb.* 8:6; 9:15; 12:24. He is Mediator, not only merely in the sense that He intervenes between God and man to sue for peace and to persuade to it, but in the sense that He is armed with full power to do all that is necessary for the actual establishment of peace. As our Surety, *Heb.* 7:22, He assumes our guilt, pays the penalty of sin, fulfils the law, and thus restores peace.

d. *Membership in the covenant.* Adults can enter the covenant as a purely legal arrangement only by faith. And when they so enter it, they at the same time gain entrance into the covenant as a communion of life. They therefore enter upon the full covenant life at once. Children of believers, however, enter the covenant as a legal arrangement by birth, but this does not necessarily mean that they also at once enter it as a communion of life, nor even that they will ever enter it in that sense. Yet the promise of God gives a reasonable assurance that the covenant life will be realized in them. As long as they do not manifest the contrary we may proceed on the assumption that they possess the new life. When they grow up, they must accept their covenant responsibilities voluntarily by a true confession of faith. Failure to do this makes them covenant breakers. From the preceding it follows that unregenerate persons may temporarily be in the covenant as a purely legal relationship, *Rom.* 9:4. They are recognized as covenant children, are subject to its requirements and share its ministrations. They receive the seal of baptism, enjoy the common blessings of the covenant, and may even partake of some special operations of the Holy Spirit. If they do not accept the corresponding responsibilities, they will be judged as breakers of the covenant.

e. *The different dispensations of the covenant.* (1) The first revelation of the covenant is found in *Gen.* 3:15, which is usually called the *protevangel* or the maternal promise. This does not yet refer to the formal establishment of the covenant. (2) The covenant with Noah is of a very general nature as a covenant with all flesh. It conveys only natural blessings, and is therefore often called the covenant of nature or of common grace. It is closely connected, however, with the covenant of grace. It is also a fruit of the grace of God and guarantees those natural and temporal blessings which are absolutely necessary for the realization of the covenant of grace. (3) The covenant with Abraham marks its formal establishment. It is the beginning of the Old Testament particularistic administration of the covenant, which is now limited to Abraham and his descendants. Faith stands out prominently as its necessary requirement, and circumcision becomes its seal. (4) The covenant at Sinai is essentially the same as that established with Abraham, but now takes in the whole nation of Israel, and thus became a national covenant. Though it strongly stresses the keeping of the law, it should not be regarded as a renewed covenant of works. The law increased the consciousness of sin, *Rom.* 3:20, and became a tutor unto Christ, *Gal.* 3:24. Passover was added as a second sacrament. (5) The new covenant, as revealed in the New Testament, *Jer.* 31:31; *Heb.* 8:8, 13, is essentially the same as that of the Old Testament, *Rom.* 4; *Gal.* 3. It now breaks through the barriers of particularism and becomes universal in the sense that its blessings are extended to people of all nations. Its blessings become fuller and more spiritual, and baptism and the Lord's Supper are substituted for the Old Testament sacraments.

To memorize. Passages bearing on:

a. *The parties of the covenant:*

Gen. 3:15. 'And I will put enmity between thee and the woman, and between thy seed and her seed: he shall bruise thy head, and thou shalt bruise his heel.'

Gen. 17:7. 'And I will establish my covenant between me and thee and thy seed after thee throughout their generations for an everlasting covenant, to be a God unto thee and to thy seed after thee.'

Exod. 19:5, 6a. 'Now therefore, if ye will obey my voice indeed, and keep my covenant, then ye shall be mine own possession from among all peoples: for all the earth is mine: and ye shall be unto me a kingdom of priests, and a holy nation.'

Jer. 31:31–33. 'Behold, the days come, saith Jehovah, that I will make a new covenant with the house of Israel, and with the house of Judah: not according to the covenant that I made with their fathers in the day that I took them by the hand to bring them out of the land of Egypt; which my covenant they brake, although I was a husband unto them, saith Jehovah. But this is the covenant that I will make with the house of Israel after those days, saith Jehovah: I will put my law in their inward parts, and in their heart will I write it; and I will be their God, and they shall be my people.'

Acts 2:39. 'For to you is the promise, and to your children, and to all that are afar off, even as many as the Lord our God shall call unto Him.'

b. *Its promises and requirements:*

See *Gen.* 17:7; *Exod.* 19:5; 6a; *Jer.* 31:33 under a. above, for the essential promise.

Gen. 15:6. 'And he (Abraham) believed in Jehovah, and He reckoned it to him for righteousness.'

Exod. 19:5. 'Now therefore, if ye will obey my voice indeed, and keep my covenant, then ye shall be mine own possession from among all peoples.'

Psa. 25:14. 'The friendship of Jehovah is with them that fear Him; and He will show them His covenant.'

Psa. 103:17, 18. 'But the lovingkindness of Jehovah is from everlasting to everlasting upon them that fear Him, and His righteousness unto children's children; to such as keep His covenant, and to those that remember His precepts to do them.'

Gal. 3:7, 9. 'Know therefore that they that are of faith, the same are sons of Abraham.... So then they that are of faith are blessed with the faithful Abraham.'

c. *Characteristics of the covenant:*

Eternal. Gen. 17:19b. 'And I will establish my covenant with him for an everlasting covenant for his seed after him.' *Isa.* 54:10. 'For the mountains may depart, and the hills be removed; but my lovingkindness shall not depart from thee, neither shall my covenant of peace be removed, saith Jehovah that hath mercy on thee.' *Isa.* 24:5. 'The earth also is polluted under the inhabitants thereof; because they have transgressed the laws, violated the statutes, broken the everlasting covenant.'

Unity. Gal. 3:7, 9 under b. above. *Rom.* 4:11. 'And he received the sign of circumcision, a seal of the righteousness of the faith which he had while he was in uncircumcision; that he might be the father of all them that believe, though they be in uncircumcision, that righteousness might be reckoned unto them.'

Testamentary. Heb. 9:17, 18. 'For a testament is of force where there hath been death; for it doth never avail while he that made it liveth. Wherefore even the first covenant hath not been dedicated without blood.'

d. *The Mediator of the covenant:*

1 Tim. 2:5. 'For there is one God, one Mediator also between God and men, Himself man, Christ Jesus.' *Heb.* 7:22. 'By so much also hath Jesus become the Surety of a better covenant.' *Heb.* 8:6. 'But now hath He obtained a ministry the more excellent by so much as He is also the

Mediator of a better covenant, which hath been enacted upon better promises.'

For Further Study:
a. Can you name some special covenants mentioned in the Bible? *Gen.* 31:44; *Deut.* 29:1; *1 Sam.* 18:3; *2 Sam.* 23:5.
b. Can you name instances of covenant breaking? *Gen.* 25:32–34, cf. *Heb.* 12:16, 17; *Exod.* 32:1–14; *Num.* 14; *Num.* 16; *Judg.* 2: 11 ff.; *1 Sam.* 2.12 ff.; *Isa.* 24:5; *Ezek.* 16:59; *Hos.* 6:7; 8:1; 10:4.
c. Did the giving of the law change the covenant essentially? *Rom.* 4:13–17; *Gal.* 3:17–24.

Questions for Review:
1. What is the covenant of redemption? By what other name is it known, and how is it related to the covenant of grace?
2. What scriptural evidence is there for it?
3. What is the official position of Christ in this covenant?
4. Was it for Christ a covenant of grace or a covenant of works?
5. Whom does Christ represent in this covenant?
6. What did the Father require of Christ, and what did He promise Him?
7. What distinction do we apply to the covenant of grace?
8. How does this affect the question, who is the second party in the covenant?
9. What is the all-embracing promise of the covenant?
10. What does God require of those who are in the covenant?
11. What are the characteristics of the covenant?
12. In what sense is the covenant unbreakable, and in what sense breakable?
13. How can you prove the unity of the covenant?
14. In what sense is it conditional, and in what sense unconditional?
15. Why can it be called a testament?
16. Where do we find the first revelation of the covenant?
17. What was the nature of the covenant with Noah?
18. How did the covenant with Abraham and the Sinaitic covenant differ?

19. What characterized the New Testament dispensation of the covenants?
20. What is the position of Christ in the covenant of grace?
21. How can adults become covenant members?
22. How do children of believers enter the covenant?
23. What is expected of them?
24. Can unregenerate persons be members of the covenant?

THE DOCTRINE OF THE PERSON AND WORK OF CHRIST

14
The Names and Natures of Christ

1. THE NAMES OF CHRIST. The most important names of Christ are the following:

a. *Jesus.* This is the Greek form of the Hebrew *Joshua, Jos.* 1:1; *Zech.* 3:1, or *Jeshua, Ezra* 2:2. Derived from the Hebrew word 'to save', it designates Christ as the Saviour, *Matt.* 1:21. Two types of Christ bore the same name in the Old Testament, namely, Joshua the son of Nun and Joshua the son of Jehozadak.

b. *Christ.* This is the New Testament form for the Old Testament 'Messiah,' which means 'the anointed one'. According to the Old Testament, prophets, *1 Kings* 19:16, priests, *Exod.* 29:7, and kings, *1 Sam.* 10:1, were anointed with oil, which symbolized the Holy Spirit. By this anointing they were set aside for their respective offices, and were qualified for them. Christ was anointed with the Holy Spirit for the threefold office of prophet, priest, and king. Historically, this anointing took place when He was conceived by the Holy Spirit and when He was baptized.

c. *Son of Man.* This name, as applied to Christ, was derived from *Dan.* 7:13. It is the name which Jesus generally applies to Himself, while others seldom use it. While it does contain an indication of the humanity of Jesus, in the light of its historical origin it points far more to His superhuman character and to His future coming with the clouds of heaven in majesty and glory, *Dan.* 7:13; *Matt.* 16:27, 28; 26:64; *Luke* 21:27.

d. *Son of God.* Christ is called 'the Son of God' in more than one sense. He is so called, because He is the second Person of the Trinity, and therefore Himself God, *Matt.* 11:27, but also because He is the appointed Messiah, *Matt.* 24:36, and because He owes His birth to the supernatural activity of the Holy Spirit, *Luke* 1:35.

e. *Lord.* Jesus' contemporaries sometimes applied this name to Jesus as a form of polite address, just as we use the word 'sir.' It is especially after the resurrection of Lord Christ that the name acquires a deeper meaning. In some passages it designates Christ as the Owner and Ruler of the Church, *Rom.* 1:7; *Eph.* 1:17, and in others it really stands for the name of God, *1 Cor.* 7:34; *Phil.* 4:4, 5.

2.   THE NATURES OF CHRIST. The Bible represents Christ as a Person having two natures, the one divine and the other human. This is the great mystery of godliness, God manifested in the flesh, *1 Tim.* 3:16.

a. *The two natures.* Since many in our day deny the deity of Christ, it is necessary to stress the Scripture proof for it. Some Old Testament passages clearly point to it, such as *Isa.* 9:6; *Jer.* 23:6; *Mic.* 5:2; *Mal.* 3:1. The New Testament proofs are even more abundant, *Matt.* 11:27; 16:16; 26:63, 64; *John* 1:1, 18; *Rom.* 9:5; *1 Cor.* 2:8; *2 Cor.* 5:10; *Phil.* 1:6; *Col.* 2:9; *Heb.* 1:1–3; *Rev.* 19:16. The *humanity* of Jesus is not called in question. In fact, the only divinity many still ascribe to Him is that of His *perfect* humanity. There is abundant proof for the humanity of Jesus. He speaks of Himself as man, *John* 8:40, and is so called by others, *Acts* 2:22; *Rom.* 5:15; 1 Cor. 15:21. He had the essential elements of human nature, namely, a body and a soul, *Matt.* 26:26, 38; *Luke* 24:39; *Heb.* 2:14. Moreover, He was subject to the ordinary laws of human development, *Luke* 2:40, 52, and to human wants and sufferings, *Matt.* 4:2; 8:24; *Luke* 22:44; *John* 4:6; 11:35; 12:27; *Heb.* 2.10, 18; *Heb.* 5:7, 8. Yet though He was a real man, *He was without sin;* He did no sin and could not sin, *John* 8:46; *2 Cor.* 5:21; *Heb.* 4:15; 9:14; *1 Pet.* 2:22; *1 John* 3:5. It was necessary that Christ should be both God and man. It was only *as man* that He could be our substitute, and could suffer and die; and only as *sinless man* that He could atone for the sins of others. And it was only *as God* that He could give His sacrifice infinite value, and bear the wrath of God so as to deliver others from it, *Psa.* 40:7–10; 130:3.

b. *The two natures united in one Person.* Christ has a human nature, but He is not a human person. The Person of the Mediator is the unchangeable Son of God. In the incarnation He did not change into a human person; neither did He adopt a human person. He simply assumed, in addition to His divine nature, a human nature, which did not develop into an independent personality, but became personal in the Person of the Son of God. After this assumption of human nature the Person or the Mediator is not only divine but *divine-human*; He is the God-man, possessing all the essential qualities of both the human and the divine nature. He has both a divine and a human consciousness, as well as a human and a divine will. This is a mystery which we cannot fathom. Scripture clearly points to the unity of the Person of Christ. It is always the same Person who speaks, whether the mind that finds utterance be human or divine, *John* 10:30; 17:5 as compared with *Matt.* 27:46; *John* 19:28. Human attributes and actions are sometimes ascribed to the Person designated by a divine title, *Acts* 20:28; *1 Cor.* 2:8; *Col.* 1:13, 14; and divine attributes and actions are sometimes ascribed to the Person designated by a human title, *John* 3:13; 6:62; *Rom.* 9:5.

c. *Some of the most important errors concerning this doctrine.* The Alogi and the Ebionites denied the *deity* of Christ in the early church. This denial was shared by the Socinians of the days of the Reformation, and by the Unitarians and Modernists of our day. In the early church Arius failed to do justice to the *full deity* of Christ and regarded Him as a demi-God, while Apollinaris did not recognize His *full humanity*, but held that the divine Logos took the place of the human spirit in Christ. The Nestorians denied the unity of the two natures in one Person, and the Eutychians failed to distinguish properly between the two natures.

To memorize. Passages to prove:

a. *The deity of Christ:*

Isa. 9:6. 'For unto us a child is born, unto us a son is given; and the government shall be upon His shoulder: and His name shall be called

Wonderful, Counsellor, Mighty God, Everlasting Father, Prince of Peace.'

Jer. 23:6. 'In His days Judah shall be saved, and Israel shall dwell safely; and this is His name whereby He shall be called: Jehovah our righteousness.'

John 1:1. 'In the beginning was the Word, and the Word was with God, and the Word was God.'

Rom. 9:5. 'Whose are the fathers, and of whom is Christ as concerning the flesh, who is over all, God blessed forever.'

Col. 2:9. 'For in Him dwelleth all the fulness of the Godhead bodily.'

b. *The humanity of Christ:*

John 8:40. 'But now ye seek to kill me, a man that hath told you the truth, which I heard from God.'

Matt. 26:38. 'Then said He unto them, My soul is exceeding sorrowful, even unto death: abide here and watch with me.'

Luke 24:39. 'See my hands and my feet, that it is I myself; handle me, and see; for a spirit hath not flesh and bones, as ye behold me having.'

Heb. 2:14. 'Since then the children are sharers in flesh and blood, He also Himself in like manner partook of the same; that through death He might bring to nought him that had the power of death, that is, the devil.'

c. *The unity of the Person:*

John 17:5. 'And now, Father, glorify Thou me with thine own self with the glory which I had with Thee before the world was.'

John 3:13. 'And no one hath ascended into heaven, but He that descended out of heaven, even the Son of Man, who is in heaven.'

1 Cor. 2:8. 'Which none of the rulers of this world hath known: for had they known it, they would not have crucified the Lord of glory.'

For Further Study:

a.   In what respect was Joshua the son of Nun a type of Christ; and in what respect Joshua the son of Jehozadak? *Zech.* 3:8, 9; *Heb.* 4:8.

b.   What do the following passages teach us respecting the anointing of Christ? *Psa.* 2:2; 45:7; *Prov.* 8:23 (see AV), *Isa.* 61:1.

c.   What divine attributes are ascribed to Christ? *Isa.* 9:6; *Prov.* 8:22–31; *Mic.* 5:2; *John* 5:26; 21:17. What divine works? *Mark* 2:5–7; *John* 1:1–3; *Col.* 1:16, 17; *Heb.* 1:1–3. What divine honour? *Matt.* 28:19; *John* 5:19–29; 14:1; *2 Cor.* 13:14.

Questions for Review:

1.   Which are the most important names of Christ? What is the meaning of each?

2.   What elements are included in Christ's anointing? When did it take place?

3.   Whence is the name 'Son of Man' derived? What does the name express?

4.   In what sense is the name 'Son of God' applied to Christ?

5.   What different meanings has the name 'Lord' as applied to Christ?

6.   What Bible proof is there for the deity and humanity of Christ?

7.   What is the nature of the Person of Christ, divine, human, or divine-human?

8.   How can the unity of the Person of Christ be proved from Scripture?

9.   What are the main errors respecting the Person of Christ?

I5

The States of Christ

We often use the words 'state' and 'condition' interchangeably. When we speak of the states of Christ, however, we use the word 'state' in a more specific sense, to denote the relation in which He stood and stands to the law. In the days of His humiliation He was a servant under the law; in His exaltation He is Lord, and as such above the law. Naturally these two states carried with them corresponding conditions of life, and these are discussed as the various stages of these states.

1.   THE STATE OF HUMILIATION. The state of humiliation consists in this, that Christ laid aside the divine majesty which was His as the sovereign Ruler of the universe, and assumed human nature in the form of a servant; that He, the supreme Lawgiver, became subject to the demands and curse of the law. *Matt.* 3:15; *Gal.* 3:13; 4:4; *Phil.* 2:6–8. This state is reflected in the corresponding condition, in which we usually distinguish several stages.

a. *The incarnation and birth of Christ.* In the incarnation the Son of God became flesh by assuming human nature, *John* 1:14; *1 John* 4:2. He really became one of the human race by being born of Mary. This would not have been true if He had brought His humanity from heaven, as the Anabaptists claim. The Bible teaches the virgin birth in *Isa.* 7:14; *Matt.* 1:20; *Luke* 1:34, 35. This wonderful birth was due to the supernatural influence of the Holy Spirit, who also kept the human nature of Christ free from the pollution of sin from its very inception, *Luke* 1:35.

b. *The sufferings of Christ.* We sometimes speak as if the sufferings of Christ were limited to His final agonies, but this is not correct. His whole life was a life of suffering. It was the servant life of the Lord of

Hosts, the life of the sinless One in a sin-cursed world. Satan assaulted Him, His people rejected Him, and His enemies persecuted Him. The sufferings of the soul were even more intense than those of the body. He was tempted by the devil, was oppressed by the world of iniquity round about Him, and staggered by the burden of sin resting upon Him – 'a man of sorrows, and acquainted with grief', *Isa*. 53:3.

c. *The death of Christ*. When we speak of the death of Christ, we naturally have in mind His physical death. He did not die as the result of an accident, nor by the hand of an assassin, but under a judicial sentence, and was thus counted with the transgressors, *Isa*. 53:12. By suffering the Roman punishment of crucifixion He died an accursed death, bearing the curse for us, *Deut*. 21:23; *Gal*. 3:13.

d. *The burial of Christ*. It might seem as if the death of Christ was the last stage of His sufferings. Did He not cry out on the cross, 'It is finished'? But these words probably refer to His active suffering. His burial certainly was a part of His humiliation, of which He as Son of God was also conscious. Man's returning to the dust is a punishment for sin, *Gen*. 3:19. That the Saviour's abode in the grave was a humiliation, is evident from *Psa*. 16:10; *Acts* 2:27, 31; 13:34, 35. It removed for us the terrors of the grave.

e. *The descent into hades*. The words of the Apostolic Confession, 'He descended into hades', are variously interpreted. Roman Catholics say that He went down into the *Limbus Patrum*, where the Old Testament saints were confined, to release them; and the Lutherans that, between His death and resurrection, He went down to hell to preach and to celebrate his victory over the powers of darkness. In all probability it is a figurative expression to denote (1) that He suffered the pangs of hell in the garden and on the cross, and (2) that He entered the deepest humiliation of the state of death, *Psa*. 16:8–10; *Eph*. 4:9.

2. THE STATE OF EXALTATION. In the state of exaltation Christ passed from under the law as a covenant obligation, having paid the penalty of sin and merited righteousness and eternal life for the sinner. Moreover, He was crowned with a corresponding honour and glory. Four stages must be distinguished here.

a. *The resurrection.* The resurrection of Christ did not consist in the mere re-union of body and soul, but especially in this, that in Him human nature, both body and soul, was restored to its original beauty and strength, and even raised to a higher level. In distinction from all those who had been raised up before Him He arose with a *spiritual* body, *1 Cor.* 15:44, 45. For that reason He can be called 'the first fruits of them that slept,' *1 Cor.* 15:20, and 'the firstborn of the dead', *Col.* 1:18; *Rev.* 1:5. The resurrection of Christ has a threefold significance: (1) It was a declaration of the Father that Christ met all the requirements of the law, *Phil.* 2:9. (2) It symbolized the justification, regeneration, and final resurrection of believers, *Rom.* 6:4, 5, 9; *1 Cor.* 6:14; 15:20–22. (3) It was the cause of our justification, regeneration, and resurrection, *Rom.* 4:25; 5:10; *Eph.* 1:20; *Phil.* 3:10; *1 Pet.* 1:3.

b. *The ascension.* The ascension was in a sense the necessary completion of the resurrection, but it also had independent significance. We have a double account of it, namely, in *Luke* 24:50,53; *Acts* 1:6–11. Paul refers to it in *Eph.* 1:20; 4:8–10; *1 Tim.* 3:16, and the Epistle to the Hebrews stresses its significance, 1:3; 4:14; 6:20; 9:24. It was a visible ascent of the Mediator, according to His human nature, from earth to heaven, a going from one place to another. It included a further glorification of the human nature of Christ. The Lutherans have a different view of it. They conceive of it as a change of condition, whereby the human nature of Jesus passed into the full enjoyment of certain divine attributes, and became permanently omnipresent. In the ascension Christ as our great high priest enters the inner sanctuary to present His sacrifice to the Father and begin His work as intercessor at the throne, *Rom.* 8:34; *Heb.* 4:14; 6:20; 9:24. He ascended to prepare a place for us, *John* 14:1–3. With Him we are already set in heavenly places, and in His ascension we have the assurance of a place in heaven, *Eph.* 2:6; *John* 17:24.

c. *The session at God's right hand.* After His ascension Christ is seated at the right hand of God, *Eph.* 1:20; *Heb.* 10:12; *1 Pet.* 3:22. Naturally, the expression 'right hand of God' cannot be taken literally, but should be understood as a figurative indication of the place of power and glory. During His session at God's right hand Christ rules and protects His church, governs the universe in its behalf, and intercedes for His people on the basis of His completed sacrifice.

d. *The physical return.* The exaltation of Christ reaches its climax when He returns to judge the living and the dead. Evidently His return will be bodily and visible, *Acts* 1:11; *Rev.* 1:7. That He will come as Judge is evident from such passages as *John* 5:22, 27; *Acts* 10:42; *Rom.* 2:16; *2 Cor.* 5:10; *2 Tim.* 4:1. The time of His second coming is not known to us. He will come for the purpose of judging the world and perfecting the salvation of His people. This will mark the complete victory of His redemptive work. *1 Cor.* 4:5; *Phil.* 3:20; *Col.* 3:4; *1 Thess.* 4:13–17; *2 Thess.* 1: 7–10; *2 Thess.* 2:1–12; *Titus* 2:13; *Rev.* 1:7.

To memorize. Passages bearing on:

a. *The state of humiliation:*

Gal. 3:13. 'Christ redeemed us from the curse of the law, having become a curse for us; for it is written, Cursed is every one that hangeth on a tree.'

Gal. 4:4, 5. 'But when the fulness of the time came, God sent forth His Son, born of a woman, born under the law, that He might redeem them that were under the law, that we might receive the adoption of sons.'

Phil. 2:6–8. 'Who, existing in the form of God, counted not the being on an equality with God a thing to be grasped, but emptied Himself, taking the form of a servant, being made in the likeness of men; and being found in fashion as a man, He humbled Himself, becoming obedient even unto death, yea, the death of the cross.'

b. *The incarnation:*

John 1:14. 'And the Word became flesh, and dwelt among us (and we beheld His glory, glory as of the only begotten from the Father), full of grace and truth.'

Rom. 8:3. 'For what the law could not do, in that it was weak through the flesh, God, sending His own Son in the likeness of sinful flesh, and for sin, condemned sin in the flesh.'

c. *The virgin birth:*

Isa. 7:14. 'Behold, a virgin shall conceive, and bear a son, and shall call His name Immanuel.'

Luke 1:35. 'And the angel answered and said unto her, The Holy Spirit shall come upon thee, and the power of the Most High shall overshadow thee: wherefore also the holy thing which is begotten shall be called the Son of God.'

d. *The descent into hades:*

Psa. 16:10. 'For Thou wilt not leave my soul to Sheol (hades, *Acts* 2:27); neither wilt Thou suffer Thy holy one to see corruption.'

Eph. 4:9. 'Now this, He ascended, what is it but that He also descended into the lower parts of the earth?'

e. *The resurrection:*

Rom. 4:25. 'Who was delivered up for our trespasses, and was raised for our justification.'

1 Cor. 15:20. 'But now hath Christ been raised from the dead, the first-fruits of them that are asleep.'

f. *The ascension:*

Luke 24:51. 'And it came to pass, while He blessed them, He parted from them, and was carried up into heaven.'

Acts 1:11. 'Who also said, Ye men of Galilee, why stand ye looking into heaven? This Jesus, who was received up from you into heaven, shall so come in like manner as ye beheld Him going into heaven.'

g. *The session:*

Eph. 1:20. 'Which He wrought in Christ, when He raised Him from the dead, and made Him to sit at His right hand in the heavenly places.'

Heb. 10:12. 'But He, when He had offered one sacrifice for sins for ever, sat down on the right hand of God.'

h. *The return:*

Acts 1:11. See above under f.

Rev. 1:7. 'Behold, He cometh with the clouds; and every eye shall see Him, and they that pierced Him; and all the tribes of the earth shall mourn over Him.'

For Further Study:

a.   What does the Old Testament tell us about the humiliation of Christ in the following passages? *Psa.* 22:6–20; 69:7–9; 20:21; *Isa.* 52:14, 15; 53:1–10; *Zech.* 11:12, 13.

b.   What was the special value of Christ's temptations for us? *Heb.* 2:18; 4:15; 5:7–9.

c.   How do the following passages prove that heaven is a place rather than a condition? *Deut.* 30:12; *Josh.* 2:11; *Psa.* 139:8: *Eccles.* 5:2; *Isa.* 66:1; *Rom* 10:6, 7.

Questions for Review:

1.   What is meant by the states of the Mediator?

2.   How would you define the states of humiliation and exaltation?

3.   What took place at the incarnation?

4.   How did Christ receive His human nature?

5.   What proof have we for the virgin birth?

6.   How was the Holy Spirit connected with the birth of Christ?

7.   Were the sufferings of Christ limited to the end of His life?

8.   Did it make any difference how Christ died?

9.   What different views are there respecting the descent into hades?

10.   What was the nature of Christ's resurrection? What change did He undergo?

11.   What was the significance of the resurrection?

12.   How would you prove that the ascension was a going from place to place?

13.   What is its significance, and how do Lutherans conceive of it?

14.   What is meant by the session at God's right hand? What does Christ do there?

15.   How will Christ return, and what is the purpose of His coming?

THE WORK OF CHRIST

16

The Offices of Christ

The Bible ascribes a threefold office to Christ, speaking of Him as Prophet, Priest, and King.

1.   THE PROPHETIC OFFICE. The Old Testament predicted the coming of Christ as a prophet, *Deut.* 18:15 (see also *Acts* 3:22–23). He speaks of Himself as a prophet in *Luke* 13:33, claims to bring a message from the Father, *John* 8:26–28; 12:49, 50; 14:10, 24, foretells future things, *Matt.* 24:3–35; *Luke* 19:41–44, and speaks with singular authority, *Matt.* 7:29. It is no wonder, therefore, that the people recognize Him as a prophet, *Matt.* 21:11, 46; *Luke* 7:16; 24:19; *John* 6:14; 7:40; 9:17.

A prophet is one who receives divine revelations in dreams, visions, or verbal communications; and passes them on to the people either orally or visibly in prophetic actions. *Exod.* 7:1; *Deut.* 18:18; *Num.* 12:6–8; *Isa.* 6; *Jer.* 1:4–10; *Ezek* 3:1–4, 17. His work may pertain to the past, the present, or the future. One of his important tasks was to interpret the moral and spiritual aspects of the law for the people. Christ functioned as prophet already in the Old Testament, *1 Pet.* 1:11; 3:18–20. He did it while He was on earth and continued it by the operation of the Holy Spirit and through the apostles after the ascension, *John* 14:26; 16:12–14; *Acts* 1:1. And even now his prophetic ministry continues through the ministry of the Word and the spiritual illumination of believers. This is the only function of Christ which is recognized in modern liberal theology.

2.   THE PRIESTLY OFFICE. The Old Testament also predicted and prefigured the priesthood of the coming Redeemer, *Psa.*
110:4; *Zech.* 6:13; *Isa.* 53. In the New Testament there is only a single
book in which He is called priest, namely, Hebrews, but there the
name is found repeatedly, 3:1; 4:14; 5:5; 6:20; 7:26; 8:1. However, other
books refer to His priestly work, *Mark* 10:45; *John* 1:29; *Rom.* 3:24, 25;
1 Cor. 5:7; *1 John* 2:2; *1 Pet.* 2:24; 3:18. While a prophet represented
God among the people, a priest represented the people before God.
Both were teachers, but while the former taught the moral, the latter
taught the ceremonial law. Moreover, the priests had the special privi-
lege of approach to God, and of speaking and acting in behalf of the
people. Hebrews 5:1, 3 teaches us that a priest is taken from among
men to be their representative, is appointed by God, is active before
God in the interests of men, and offers gifts and sacrifices for sins. He
also makes intercession for the people.

The priestly work of Christ was, first of all, to bring a sacrifice for
sin. The Old Testament sacrifices were types pointing forward to the
great sacrifice of Christ, *Heb.* 9:23, 24; 10:1; 13:11, 12. Hence Christ
is also called 'the Lamb of God,' *John* 1:29, and 'our passover,' *1 Cor.*
5:7. The New Testament speaks very clearly of the priestly work of
Christ in numerous passages: *Mark* 10:45; *John* 1:29; *Rom.* 3:24, 25;
5:6–8; *1 Cor.* 5:7; 15:3; *Gal.* 1:4; *Eph.* 5:2; *1 Pet.* 2:24; 3:18; *1 John*
2:2; 4:10; *Rev.* 5:12. The references are most frequent in the Epistle
to the Hebrews, 5:1–10; 7:1–28; 9:11–15, 24–28; 10:11–14,19–22;
12:24; 13:12.

Besides bringing the great sacrifice for sins, Christ as Priest also
makes intercession for His people. He is called our *parakletos* by
implication in *John* 14:16, and explicitly in *1 John* 2:2. The term means
'one who is called in to help, an advocate, one who pleads the cause
of another'. The New Testament refers to Christ as our intercessor
in *Rom.* 8:34; *Heb.* 7:25; 9:24; *1 John* 2:1. His intercessory work is
based on His sacrifice, and is not limited, as is sometimes thought, to
intercessory prayer. He presents His sacrifice to God, on the ground
of it claims all spiritual blessings for His people, defends them against
the charges of Satan, the law, and conscience, secures forgiveness for
everything justly charged against them, and sanctifies their worship

and service through the operation of the Holy Spirit. This intercessory work is limited in character; it has reference only to the elect, but includes all the elect, whether they are already believers or still live in unbelief, *John* 17:9, 20.

3.   THE KINGLY OFFICE. As Son of God Christ naturally shares in the universal dominion of God. In distinction from this we speak of a kingship that was conferred on Him *as Mediator*. This kingship is twofold, namely, His spiritual kingship over the Church, and His kingship over the universe.

a. *His spiritual kingship.* The Bible speaks of this in many places, *Psa.* 2:6; 132:11; *Isa.* 9:6, 7; *Mic.* 5:2; *Zech.* 6:13; *Luke* 1:33; 19:38; *John* 18:36, 37; *Acts* 2:30–36. The kingship of Christ is His royal rule over His people. It is called *spiritual*, because it relates to a spiritual realm, is established in the hearts and lives of believers, has a spiritual end in view, the salvation of sinners, and is administered by spiritual means, the Word and the Spirit. It is exercised largely in the gathering, the government, the protection, and the perfection of the Church. This kingship as well as the realm over which it extends is called in the New Testament 'the kingdom of God' or 'the kingdom of heaven.'

In the strict sense of the word only believers, members of the invisible church, are citizens of the kingdom. But the term 'kingdom of God' is sometimes used in a broader sense, as including all who live under the proclamation of the gospel, all who have a place in the visible church, *Matt.* 13:24–30, 47–50. This kingdom of God is on the one hand a *present*, spiritual reality in the hearts and lives of men, *Matt.* 12:28; *Luke* 17:21; *Col.* 1:13; but on the other hand a *future* hope, which will not be realized until the return of Jesus Christ, *Matt.* 7:21; *Luke* 22:29; *1 Cor.* 15:50; *2 Tim.* 4:18; *2 Pet.* 1:11. The future kingdom will be essentially the same as the present, namely, the rule of God established and acknowledged in the hearts of men. It will differ, however, in that it will be *visible* and *perfect*. Some are of the opinion that this kingship of Christ will cease at His return, but the Bible would seem to teach explicitly that it will endure for ever, *Psa.* 45:6; 72:17; 89:36, 37; *Isa.* 9:6; *Dan.* 2:44; *2 Sam.* 7:13, 16; *Luke* 1:33; *2 Pet.* 1:11.

b. *His universal kingship.* After the resurrection Christ said to His disciples: 'All authority hath been given unto Me in heaven and on earth.' *Matt.* 28:18. The same truth is taught in *1 Cor.* 15:27; *Eph.* 1:20–22. This kingship should not be confused with the original kingship of Christ *as the Son of God,* though it pertains to the same realm. It is the kingship of the universe entrusted to Christ *as Mediator* in behalf of His church. As Mediator He now guides the destiny of individuals and nations, controls the life of the world and makes it subservient to His redemptive purpose, and protects His church against the dangers to which it is exposed in the world. This kingship will last until the victory over the enemies of the kingdom of God is complete. When the end is accomplished, it will be returned to the Father, *1 Cor.* 15:24–28.

To Memorize. Passages pointing to:

a. *Christ as prophet:*

Deut. 18:18. 'I will raise them up a prophet from among their brethren, like unto thee; and I will put my words in his mouth, and he shall speak unto them all that I shall command him.'

Luke 7:16. 'And fear took hold on all; and they glorified God, saying, A great prophet is arisen among us: and God hath visited His people.'

b. *Christ as priest:*

Psa. 110:4. 'Jehovah hath sworn, and will not repent: Thou art a priest for ever after the order of Melchizedek.'

Heb. 3:1. 'Wherefore, holy brethren, partakers of a heavenly calling, consider the Apostle and High Priest of our confession, even Jesus.'

Heb. 4:14. 'Having then a great high priest, who hath passed through the heavens, Jesus the Son of God, let us hold fast our confession.'

c. *His characteristics as priest:*

Heb. 5:1, 5. 'For every high priest, being taken from among men, is appointed for men in things pertaining to God, that he may offer both gifts and sacrifices for sins. . . . So Christ also glorified not Himself to be made a high priest, but He that spake unto Him, Thou art My Son, this day have I begotten Thee.'

d. *His sacrificial work:*

Isa. 53:5. 'But He was wounded for our transgressions, He was bruised for our iniquities; the chastisement of our peace was upon Him; and with his stripes we are healed.'

Mark 10:45. 'For the Son of Man also came not to be ministered unto, but to minister, and to give His soul a ransom for many.'

John 1:29. 'Behold, the Lamb of God, that taketh away the sin of the world.'

1 Pet. 2:24. 'Who His own self bare our sins in His body upon the tree, that we, having died unto sins, might live unto righteousness.'

1 John 2:2. 'And He is the propitiation for our sins; and not for ours only, but for the whole world.'

e. *His intercessory work:*

Rom. 8:34. 'It is Christ Jesus that died, yea rather, that was raised from the dead, who is at the right hand of God, who also maketh intercession for us.'

Heb. 7:25. 'Wherefore also He is able to save to the uttermost them that draw near unto God through Him, seeing He ever liveth to make intercession for them.'

1 John 2:1b. 'And if any man sin, we have an Advocate with the Father, Jesus Christ the righteous.'

f. *Christ as king of Zion:*

Psa. 2:6. 'Yet I have set my king upon my holy hill of Zion.'

Isa. 9:7. 'Of the increase of His government and of peace there shall be no end upon the throne of David, and upon His kingdom, to establish it, and to uphold it with justice and with righteousness from henceforth even for ever.'

Luke 1:32,33. 'He shall be great, and shall be called the Son of the Most High: and the Lord God shall give unto Him the throne of His father David: and He shall reign over the house of Jacob for ever; and of His kingdom there shall be no end.'

g. *Christ as king of the universe:*

Matt. 28:18. 'And Jesus came to them and spake unto them, saying. All authority hath been given unto me in heaven and on earth.'

Eph. 1: 22. 'And He put all things in subjection under His feet and gave Him to be head over all things to the Church.'

1 Cor. 15:25. 'For He must reign, till He hath put all His enemies under His feet.'

For Further Study:

a.   What do the following passages tell us respecting the nature of the prophetic work? *Exod.* 7:1; *Deut.* 18:18; *Ezek.* 3:17.

b.   What Old Testament types of Christ are indicated in the following passages? *John* 1:29; *1 Cor.* 5:7; *Heb.* 3:1; 4:14; 8:3-5; 9:13, 14; 10:1–14; 13:11, 12.

c.   What do the following passages teach us respecting the kingdom of God? *John* 3:3, 5; 18:36,37; *Rom.* 14:17; *1 Cor.* 4:20.

Questions for Review:

1.   What threefold office has Christ?
2.   What is a prophet, and what proof is there that Christ is a prophet?
3.   How did Christ function as prophet in various periods of history?
4.   What is a priest in distinction from a prophet? How did their teaching differ?
5.   What Scriptural proof is there for the priestly character of Christ?
6.   What are the characteristics of a priest?
7.   What was the nature of Christ's sacrificial work? How was it foreshadowed in the Old Testament?
8.   In what does the work of Christ as intercessor consist?
9.   For whom does Christ intercede?
10.   What is the spiritual kingship of Christ, and over what realms does it extend?
11.   How is the present kingdom of Christ related to His future kingdom?
12.   How long will His spiritual kingship last?
13.   What is the nature and purpose of His universal kingdom?
14.   How long will this last?

17
The Atonement Through Christ

There is one part of Christ's priestly work that calls for further consideration, namely, the atonement.

1. THE MOVING CAUSE AND NECESSITY OF THE ATONEMENT. It is sometimes represented as if the moving cause of the atonement lay in Christ's sympathy for sinners. God in His anger, it is said, was bent on the sinner's destruction, but the loving Christ steps in between and saves the sinner. Christ receives all the glory, and the Father is robbed of His honour. The Bible teaches us that the atonement finds its moving cause in the good pleasure of God, *Isa.* 53:10; *Luke* 2:14; *Eph.* 1:6–9; *Col.* 1:19, 20. It is best to say that the atonement is rooted in the love and justice of God: love offered sinners a way of escape, and justice demanded that the requirements of the law should be met, *John* 3:16; *Rom.* 3:24–26. Some deny the *necessity* of the atonement, and hold that God could have pardoned the sinner without receiving any satisfaction. The Bible teaches, however, that a righteous and holy God cannot simply overlook sin, but reacts against it, *Exod.* 20:5; 23:7; *Psa.* 5:5, 6; *Nah.* 1:2; *Rom.* 1:18, 32. Moreover, He had pronounced the sentence of death upon the sinner, *Gen.* 3:3; *Rom.* 6:23.

2. THE NATURE OF THE ATONEMENT. The following particulars should be noted here.

a. *It served to render satisfaction to God.* It is often said that the atonement served primarily, if not exclusively, to influence the sinner, to awaken repentance in his heart, and thus to bring him back to God. But this is clearly wrong, for if a person offends another, amends should be made, not to the offender, but to the offended party. This means that the primary purpose of the atonement was to reconcile God to the sinner. The reconciliation of the sinner to God may be regarded as its secondary purpose.

b. *It was a vicarious atonement.* God might have demanded a personal atonement of the sinner, but the latter would not have been able to render it. In view of this fact God graciously ordained that Christ should take the place of man as his *vicar* or *substitute.* Christ as our vicar atoned for the sin of mankind by bearing the penalty of sin and meeting the demands of the law, and thus wrought an eternal redemption for man. For that reason we speak of the atonement as a *vicarious* atonement. The offended party Himself made provision for the atonement in this case. The Old Testament sacrifice prefigured the atoning work of Christ, *Lev.* 1:4; 4:20, 31, 35; 5:10, 16; 6:7; 17:11. We are taught that our sins were laid upon Christ, *Isa.* 53:6, He bore them, *John* 1:29, *Heb.* 9:28, and gave His life for sinners, *Mark* 10:45; *Gal* 1:4; *1 Pet.* 3:18.

c. *It included Christ's active and passive obedience.* It is customary to distinguish a twofold obedience of Christ. His *active obedience* consists in all that He did to observe the law in behalf of sinners, as a condition for obtaining eternal life; and His *passive obedience* in all that He suffered in paying the penalty of sin and discharging the debt of His people. But while we distinguish these two, we should never separate them. Christ was active also in His suffering, and passive also in His submission to the law. Scripture teaches us that He paid the penalty of the law, *Isa.* 53:8; *Rom.* 4:25; *Gal.* 3:13; *1 Pet.* 2:24, and merited eternal life for the sinner, *Rom.* 8:4; 10:4; *2 Cor.* 5:21; *Gal.* 4:4–7.

3. THE EXTENT OF THE ATONEMENT. Roman Catholics, Lutherans, and Arminians of every description regard the atonement of Christ as universal. This does not mean that in their estimation all men will be saved, but merely that Christ suffered and died *for the purpose of saving all without any exception. They admit that the intended effect is not achieved.* Christ did not actually save, but made salvation possible for all. Their actual redemption is dependent on their own choice. Reformed Churches on the other hand believe in a limited atonement. Christ suffered and died *for the purpose of saving*

only the elect, and that purpose is actually accomplished. Christ not merely made salvation possible but really saves to the uttermost every one of those for whom he laid down His life, *Luke* 19:10; *Rom.* 5:10; *2 Cor.* 5:21; *Gal.* 1:4; *Eph.* 1:7. The Bible indicates that Christ laid down His life for His people, *Matt.* 1:21, for His sheep, *John* 10:11, 15, for the church, *Acts* 20:28; *Eph.* 5:25–27, or for the elect, *Rom.* 8:32–35. If the Bible sometimes says that Christ died *for the world, John* 1:29; *1 John* 2:2; 4:14, or *for all, 1 Tim.* 2:6; *Titus* 2:11; *Heb.* 2:9, this evidently means that He died for people of all nations of the world, or (in some instances) for all kinds or classes of people.

To memorize. Passages bearing on:

a. *The cause of the atonement:*
Isa. 53:10. 'Yet it pleased Jehovah to bruise Him, He hath put Him to grief: when Thou shalt make His soul an offering for sin, He shall see His seed, He shall prolong his days, and the pleasure of Jehovah shall prosper in His hand.'
Col. 1:19, 20. 'For it was the good pleasure of the Father that in Him should all the fullness dwell; and through Him to reconcile all things unto Himself, having made peace through the blood of His cross.'

b. *Vicarious atonement:*
Isa. 53:6. 'All we like sheep have gone astray; we have turned every one to his own way; and Jehovah hath laid on Him the iniquity of us all.'
Mark 10:45. 'For the Son also came not to be ministered unto, but to minister, and to give His life a ransom for many.'
2 Cor. 5:21. 'Him who knew no sin He made to be sin on our behalf; that we might become the righteousness of God in Him.'
1 Pet. 2:24. 'Who His own self bare our sins in His body upon the tree, that we having died unto sins, might live unto righteousness.'

c. *Active obedience and the gift of eternal life:*
Matt. 3:15. 'But Jesus answering said unto him, Suffer it now: for thus it becometh us to fulfill all righteousness.'
Matt. 5:17. 'Think not that I came to destroy the law or the prophets: I came not to destroy, but to fulfil.'

Gal. 4:4, 5. 'But when the fullness of time came, God sent forth His Son, born of a woman, born under the law, that He might redeem them that were under the law, that we might receive the adoption of sons.'

John 10:28. 'And I give unto them eternal life, and they shall never perish, and no one shall snatch them out of my hand.'

Rom. 6:23. 'For the wages of sin is death; but the free gift of God is eternal life in Jesus our Lord.'

d. *Limited atonement:*

Matt. 1:21. 'And she shall bring forth a son: and thou shalt call His name Jesus; for it is He that shall save His people from their sins.'

John 10:26–28. 'But ye believe not, because ye are not of my sheep. My sheep hear my voice, and I know them, and they follow me: and I give unto them eternal life; and they shall never perish, and no one shall snatch them out of my hand.'

Acts 20:28. 'Take heed unto yourselves, and to all the flocks, in which the Holy Spirit hath made you bishops, to feed the Church of the Lord which He purchased with His own blood.'

For Further Study:

a.   What is the difference between atonement and reconciliation?

b.   How do the following passages prove the vicarious nature of Old Testament sacrifices? *Lev.* 1:4; 3:2; 4:15; 16:21, 22.

c.   Does *John* 17:9 teach us anything respecting the extent of the atonement?

Questions for Review:

1.   What was the moving cause of the atonement?

2.   Why was the atonement necessary?

3.   What was the primary purpose of the atonement?

4.   What is the difference between personal and vicarious atonement?

5.   How was Christ's vicarious atonement prefigured in the Old Testament?

6.   What Scripture proof is there for it?

7. What is the difference between the active and passive obedience of Christ?

8. What did each one of these effect?

9. What difference of opinion is there respecting the extent of the atonement?

10. What is meant by universal atonement, and who teach it?

11. What is limited atonement, and what Scripture proof is there for it?

12. What objections are raised against this, and how can they be answered?

THE DOCTRINE OF THE APPLICATION OF THE WORK OF REDEMPTION

18

The Common Operations of the Holy Spirit: Common Grace

The study of the work or redemption wrought by Christ is naturally followed by a discussion of the application of this redemption to the hearts and lives of sinners by the *special* operation of the Holy Spirit. Before taking this up a brief chapter will be devoted to the *general* operations of the Holy Spirit, as these are seen in commongrace.

1. NATURE OF COMMON GRACE. When we speak of a common grace, we have in mind either, (a) *those general operations of the Holy Spirit whereby He, without renewing the heart, exercises such a moral influence on man that sin is restrained, order is maintained in social life, and civil righteousness is promoted; or* (b) *those general blessings which God imparts to all men without any distinction as He sees fit.* In distinction from the Arminians we maintain that common grace does not enable the sinner to perform any spiritual good, nor to turn to God in faith and repentance. It can be resisted by man, and is always more or less resisted, and at best affects only the externals of social, civil, moral, and religious life. While Christ died for the purpose of saving only the elect, nevertheless the whole human race, including the impenitent and the reprobate, derive great benefits from His death. The blessings of common grace may be regarded as indirect fruits of the atoning work of Christ.

2.   MEANS OF COMMON GRACE. Several means may be distinguished: (a) The most important of these is *the light of God's general revelation*. Without this all other means would be impossible and ineffective It lightens every man, and serves to guide the conscience of the natural man. (b) *Human governments also serve this purpose.* According to our Confession[1] they are instituted to curb evil tendencies, and to promote good order and decency. (c) *Public opinion is another important means wherever it is in harmony with the law of God.* It has a tremendous influence on the conduct of men who are very sensitive to the judgment of public opinion. (d) *Finally, divine punishments and rewards also serve to encourage moral goodness in the world.* The punishments often check the sinful deeds of men, and the rewards spur them on to do what is good and right.

3.   THE EFFECTS OF COMMON GRACE. The following effects may be ascribed to the operation of common grace: (a) *The execution of the sentence of death on man is deferred.* God did not at once fully execute the sentence of death on the sinner, and does not do so now, but gives him time for repentance, *Rom.* 2:4; *2 Pet.* 3:9. (b) *Sin is restrained in the lives of individuals and nations.* The corruption that entered human life through sin is retarded and not yet permitted to complete its destructive work, *Gen.* 20:6; 31:7; *Job.* 1:12; 2:6. (c) *Man still has some sense of the true, the good, and the beautiful, appreciates this in a measure, and reveals a desire for truth, morality, and certain forms of religion, Rom.* 2:14, 15; *Acts* 17:22. (d) *The natural man is still able to perform natural good or civil righteousness,* works that are outwardly in harmony with the law, though without spiritual value, *2 Kings* 10.29, 30; 12:2; 14:3; *Luke* 6:33. (e) *All men receive numerous undeserved blessings from God, Psa.* 145:9, 15,16; *Matt.* 5.44,45; *Luke* 6:35,36; *Acts* 14:16,17, *1 Tim.* 4.10.

To memorize. Passages proving:

a. *A general striving of the Spirit with men:*
Gen. 6.3. 'And Jehovah said, My Spirit shall not strive with man for ever, for that he also is flesh.'

[1] This is a reference to the *Belgic Confession*, Article 36.

Isa. 63:10. 'But they rebelled, and grieved His Holy Spirit; therefore He was turned to be their enemy, and Himself fought against them.'

Rom. 1:28. 'And even as they refused to have God in their knowledge, God gave them up unto a reprobate mind, to do those things which are not fitting.'

b. *Restraint of sin:*

Gen. 20.6. 'And God said unto him (Abimelech) in the dream, Yea, I know that in the integrity of thy heart thou hast done and I also withheld thee from sinning against me.'

Gen. 31:7. 'And your father hath deceived me, and changed any wages ten times; but God suffered him not to hurt me.'

Psa. 105.14. 'He suffered no man to do them wrong; yea, He reproved kings for their sakes.'

c. *Good works on the part of unregenerate:*

2 Kings 10:30. 'And Jehovah said unto Jehu, because thou hast done well in executing that which is right in mine eyes, and hast done unto the house of Ahab according to all that was in my heart thy sons of the fourth generation shall sit on the throne of Israel.' See also verse 31.

Luke 6.33. 'And if ye do good to them that do good to you, what thank have ye? for even sinner do the same.'

Rom. 2:14, 15. 'For when Gentiles that have not the law do by nature the things of the law, these not having the law, are the law unto themselves; in that they show the work of the law written in their hearts.'

d. *Unmerited blessings on all men:*

Psa. 145:9. 'Jehovah is good to all; and His tender mercies are over all His works.'

Matt. 5:44, 45. 'But I say unto you, Love your enemies, and pray for them that persecute you; that ye may be sons of your Father who is in heaven; for He maketh His sun to rise on the evil and the good, and sendeth rain on the just and the unjust.'

1 Tim. 4:10. 'For to this end we labour and strive, because we have our hope set on the living God, who is the Saviour of all men, especially of them that believe.'

For Further Study:

a. Which are the three points emphasized by the Reformed Church as to common grace?

b. How do *Matt.* 21:26, 46; *Mark* 14:2 show the restraining influence of public opinion?

c. How do *Rom.* 1:24, 26.,28, and *Heb.* 6:4–6 prove common grace?

Questions for Review:

1. What is common grace?
2. What is the Reformed view in distinction from the Arminian?
3. Does common grace have any spiritual and saving effect?
4. Is it in any way connected with the redemptive work of Christ?
5. By what means does common grace work?
6. What are the effects of common grace?

19

Calling and Regeneration

1.   CALLING. Calling in general may be defined as that *gracious act of God whereby He invites sinners to accept the salvation that is offered in Christ Jesus*. It may be either external or internal.

a. *External calling*. The Bible speaks of this or refers to it in several passages, *Matt.* 28:19; 22:14; *Luke* 14:16–24; *Acts* 13:46; *2 Thess.* 1:8; *1 John* 5:10. It consists in *the presentation and offering of salvation in Christ to sinners, together with an earnest exhortation to accept Christ by faith in order to obtain the forgiveness of sins and eternal life*. From the definition it already appears that it contains three elements, namely, (1) *A presentation of the gospel facts and ideas;* (2) *an invitation to repent and believe in Jesus Christ*, and (3) *a promise of forgiveness and salvation.* The promise is always conditional; its fulfilment can be expected only in the way of true faith and repentance.

The external call is *universal* in the sense that it comes to all men to whom the gospel is preached. It is not limited to any age or nation or class of men, and comes to the reprobate as well as to the elect, *Isa.* 45:22; 55:1; *Ezek.* 3:19; *Joel* 2:32; *Matt.* 22:2–8, 14; *Rev.* 22:17.

Naturally this call, as coming from God, is *seriously meant*. He calls sinners in good faith, earnestly desires that they accept the invitation, and in all sincerity promises eternal life to those who repent and believe. *Num.* 23:19; *Psa.* 81:13–16; *Prov.* 1:24; *Isa.* 1:18–20; *Ezek.* 18:23, 32; 33:11; *Matt.* 23:37; *2 Tim.* 2:13. In the external call God maintains His claim on the sinner. If man does not accept the call, he slights the claim of God and thus increases his guilt. It is also the appointed means by which God gathers the elect out of all the nations of the world, *Rom.* 10:14–17, and should be regarded as a blessing for sinners, though they may turn it into a curse, *Isa.* 1:18–20; *Ezek.* 3:18,19; *Amos* 8:11; *Matt.*

11:20–24; 23:37. Finally, it also serves to justify God in the condemnation of sinners. If they despise the offer of salvation, their guilt stands out in the clearest light, *John* 5:39; 40, *Rom.* 3:5, 6, 19.

b. *Internal calling.* While we distinguish two aspects of the calling of God, this calling is really one. The internal call is really the external call made effective by the operation of the Holy Spirit. It always comes to the sinner through the Word of God, *savingly applied by the operation of the Holy Spirit, 1 Cor.* 1:23, 24. In distinction from the external call, it is a *powerful calling* that is effectual unto salvation, *Acts* 13:48; *1 Cor.* 1:23, 24. Moreover, it is a calling *without repentance*, one that is not subject to change, and is never withdrawn, *Rom.* 11:29. The person called will surely be saved. The Spirit operates through the preaching of the Word by making its persuasions effective, so that man listens to the voice of his God. It addresses itself to the understanding enlightened by the Holy Spirit, so that man is conscious of it. And it is always directed to a certain end. It is a calling to the fellowship of Jesus Christ, *1 Cor.* 1:9, to inherit blessing, *1 Pet.* 3:9, to liberty, *Gal.* 5:13, to peace, *1 Cor.* 7:15; to holiness, *1 Thess.* 4:7; to one hope, *Eph.* 4:4, to eternal life, *1 Tim.* 6:12, and to God's kingdom and glory, *1 Thess.* 2:12.

2.   REGENERATION. Divine calling and regeneration stand in the closest possible relation to each other. With respect to regeneration several points deserve consideration:

a. *Its nature.* The word 'regeneration' is not always used in the same sense. Our Confession[1] uses it in a broad sense, as including even conversion. At present it has a more restricted meaning. In the most restricted sense it denotes *that act of God by which the principle of the new life is implanted in man, and the governing disposition of the soul is made holy.* In a slightly more comprehensive sense it designates in addition to the preceding, *the new birth or the first manifestation of the new life.* It is a *fundamental* change in the principle of life and the governing disposition of the soul, *and therefore affects the whole man,*

---

[1] This is a reference to the *Belgic Confession*, Article 25.

1 Cor. 2:14; *2 Cor.* 4:6; *Phil.* 2:13; *1 Pet.* 1:8. It is completed in a moment of time, and is not a gradual process like sanctification. Through it we pass from death into life, *1 John* 3:14. It is a secret and inscrutable work of God that is never *directly* perceived by man, but can be known only *by its effects.*

b. *Its author.* God is the author of regeneration. Scripture represents it as the work of the Holy Spirit, *John* 1:13; *Acts* 16:14; *John* 3:5, 8. Over against the Arminians we maintain that it is exclusively the work of the Spirit of God, and not in part the work of man. There is no co- operation of God and man in the work of regeneration, as there is in the work of conversion. Moreover, it should be said that regeneration in the most restricted sense of the word, that is, as the implanting of the new life, is a *direct* and *immediate* work of the Holy Spirit. It is a *creative* work in which for that very reason the word of the gospel cannot very well be used as an instrument. It may be said that James 1:18 and 1 Pet. 1:23 prove that the word of preaching is used as an instrument in regeneration, but these passages refer to regeneration in a broader sense, as including the new birth. In that more inclusive sense regeneration is undoubtedly wrought through the instrumentality of the Word.

c. *Its necessity and place in the order of salvation.* Scripture leaves no doubt as to the absolute necessity of regeneration, but asserts this in the clearest terms, *John* 3:3, 5, 7; *1 Cor.* 2:14; *Gal.* 6:15. This follows from the fact that we are by nature dead in trespasses and sin, and must be endowed with new spiritual life, in order to enjoy the divine favour and communion with God. The question is often raised which of the two is first, calling or regeneration. In answer to this it may be said that in the case of adults external calling usually precedes or coincides with regeneration in the restricted sense. Regeneration, as the implanting of the new life, precedes internal calling, and internal calling precedes regeneration in the broader sense, or the new birth. We find the greater part of this order indicated in the record of the conversion of Lydia, *Acts* 16:14, 'And a certain woman named Lydia, a seller of purple, of the city of Thyatira, one that worshipped God, heard us (external call); whose heart the Lord opened (regeneration in the restricted sense) to give heed unto the things which were spoken by Paul (internal call).'

To memorize. Passages proving:

a. *External calling:*
Mark 16:15, 16. 'And He said unto them, Go ye into all the world, and preach the gospel to the whole creation ['every creature,' AV]. He that believeth and is baptized shall be saved; but he that disbelieveth shall be condemned.'
Matt. 22:14. 'For many are called, but few chosen.'
Acts 13:46. 'And Paul and Barnabas spake out boldly, and said, It was necessary that the word of God should first be spoken to you. Seeing ye thrust it from you, and judge yourselves unworthy of eternal life, lo, we turn to the Gentiles.'

b. *Calling of the reprobate:*
Prov. 1:24–26. 'Because I have called, and ye have refused; I have stretched out my hand, and no man hath regarded; but ye have set at nought all my counsel, and would none of my reproof: I also will laugh in the day of your calamity; I will mock when your fear cometh.'
1 Pet. 3:19, 20a. 'In which also He (Christ) went and preached unto the spirits in prison, that aforetime were disobedient, when the long-suffering of God waited in the days of Noah.'
Compare also the parables in *Matt.* 22:1–8, 14; *Luke* 14:16–24.

c. *Seriousness of this calling:*
Prov. 1:24–26, see above under b.
Ezek. 18:23, 32. 'Have I any pleasure in the death of the wicked? said the Lord Jehovah; and not rather that he should return from his way and live? ... For I have no pleasure in the death of him that dieth, saith the Lord Jehovah: wherefore turn yourselves, and live.' See also 33:11.
Matt. 23:37. 'O Jerusalem, Jerusalem, that killeth the prophets, and stoneth them that are sent unto her! how often would I have gathered thy children together, even as a hen gathereth her chickens under her wings, and ye would not.'

d. *The necessity of regeneration:*

Jer. 13:23. 'Can the Ethiopian change his skin, or the leopard his spots? Then may ye also do good, that are accustomed to do evil.'

John 3:3, 7 'Jesus answered and said unto him, Verily, verily, I say unto thee, Except one be born anew, he cannot see the kingdom of God . . . Marvel not that I said unto thee, Ye must be born anew.'

e. *Regeneration and the Word.*

James 1:18. 'Of His own will He brought us forth by the word of truth, that we should be a kind of first fruits of His creatures.'

1 Pet. 1:23. 'Having been begotten again, not of corruptible seed, but of incorruptible, through the word of God, which liveth and abideth.'

For Further Study:

a. Is calling a work of one Person of the Trinity or of all three? *1 Cor.* 1:9; *1 Thess.* 2:12; *Matt.* 11:28; *Luke* 5:32; *Matt.* 10:20; *Acts* 5:31, 32.

b. Is the word 'regeneration' used in the Bible? *Titus* 3:5. What other terms does it use to express this idea? *John* 3:3, 5, 7, 8; *2 Cor.* 5:17; *Eph.* 2:5; *Col.* 2:13; *James* 1:18; *1 Pet.* 1:23.

c. Does *Titus* 3:5 prove that we are regenerated by baptism? If not, how would you explain it?

Questions for Review:

1. What do we mean by calling?
2. How do external and internal calling differ?
3. What elements are included in external calling?
4. In what sense is it universal?
5. What purpose does it serve?
6. How is the internal related to the external calling?
7. Are we conscious of it?
8. To what end is it directed?
9. What different meanings has the word 'regeneration'?
10. What is it in the most restricted sense?
11. What is the nature of the change wrought in regeneration?

12.   Is regeneration a work of God alone or of God and man?
13.   Is the Word used as an instrument in regeneration?
14.   Is regeneration absolutely necessary? Prove this.
15.   What is the order of calling and regeneration?

20
Conversion: Repentance and Faith

When the change wrought in regeneration begins to manifest itself in the conscious life, we speak of conversion.

1.   CONVERSION IN GENERAL. The Bible does not always speak of conversion in the same sense. The conversion we have in mind here may be defined as *that act of God whereby He causes the regenerated, in their conscious life, to turn to Him in faith and repentance.* From this definition it already appears that God is the author of conversion. This is clearly taught in Scripture, *Acts* 11:18; *2 Tim.* 2:25. The new life of regeneration does not of itself issue in a conscious change of life, but only through a special operation of the Holy Spirit, *John* 6:44; *Phil.* 2:13. But while in regeneration God only works and man is passive, in conversion man is called upon to co-operate, *Isa.* 55.7; *Jer.* 18:11; *Acts* 2:38; 17:30. But even so man can only work with the power which God imparts to him.

Like regeneration conversion too consists in a momentary change, and is not a process like sanctification; but in distinction from regeneration it is a change in the conscious rather than in the unconscious life of man. While conversion is necessary in the case of all adults, *Ezek.* 33:11; *Matt.* 18:3, it need not appear in the life of each one of them as a sharply marked crisis. The Bible mentions instances of conversion, such as Naaman, *2 Kings* 5:15; Manasseh, *2 Chron.* 33:12, 13; Zacchaeus, *Luke* 19:8, 9; the eunuch, *Acts* 8:30 ff.; Cornelius, *Acts* 10.44 ff.; Paul, *Acts* 9:5 ff.; Lydia, *Acts* 16:14, and so on. Besides this it also speaks of *a national conversion,* as in *Jon.* 3:10, a temporary conversion, which includes no change of heart, *Matt.* 13:20, 21; *1 Tim.* 1:19, 20; *2 Tim.* 4:10; *Heb.* 6:4–6, and a repeated conversion,

Luke 22:32; *Rev.* 2:5, 16, 21, 22; 3:3, 19. This is not a repetition of conversion in the strict sense of the word, which does not admit of repetition, but a revived activity of the new life after it has suffered eclipse. Conversion comprises two elements, the one negative and the other positive, namely repentance and faith, which call for separate discussion.

2.   REPENTANCE, THE NEGATIVE ELEMENT OF CONVERSION. Repentance looks to the past, and may be defined as *that change wrought in the conscious life of the sinner by which he turns away from sin.* It includes three elements, namely, (a) *an intellectual element,* in which the past life is viewed as a life of sin, involving personal guilt, defilement, and helplessness; (b) *an emotional element,* a sense of sorrow for sin as committed against a holy and just God; and (c) *an element of the will,* consisting in a change of purpose, an inward turning from sin and a disposition to seek pardon and cleansing. *Rom.* 3:20; *2 Cor.* 7:9, 10; *Rom.* 2:4. It is wrought in man primarily by the law of God. Roman Catholics have an external conception of repentance. According to them it comprises a sorrow, not for inborn sin, but for personal transgressions, which may merely result from the fear of eternal punishment; a confession made to the priest, who can forgive sin; and a measure of satisfaction by external deeds of penance, such as fastings, scourgings, pilgrimages, and so on. The Bible, on the other hand, views repentance wholly as an inward act, an act of real sorrow on account of sin, and does not confuse this with the change of life in which it results.

3.   FAITH, THE POSITIVE ELEMENT OF CONVERSION. In distinction from repentance, faith has a forward look.

a. *Different kinds of faith.* The Bible does not always speak of faith in the same sense. It refers to a *historical faith,* consisting in an intellectual acceptance of the truth of Scripture without any real moral or spiritual response. Such a faith does not take the truth seriously and shows no real moral or spiritual interest in it. *Acts* 26:27, 28; *James* 2:19. It also speaks of a *temporal faith,* which embraces the truths of religion with some promptings of conscience and a stirring of the affections, but is not rooted in a regenerated heart. It is called temporal faith, *Matt.* 13:20, 21, because it has no abiding character and fails to maintain itself in days of trial and persecution. See also *Heb.* 6:4–6; *1 Tim.* 1:19, 20; *1 John* 2:19. Moreover, it makes mention of a *miraculous faith*, that is a person's conviction that a miracle will be performed by him or in his behalf. *Matt.* 8:11–13; 17:20; *Mark* 16:17, 18; *John* 11:22, 40; *Acts* 14:9. This faith may or may not be accompanied with saving faith. Finally, it not only names, but stresses the necessity of, *saving faith*. It has its seat in the heart and is rooted in the regenerated life. Its seed is implanted in regeneration and gradually blossoms into an active faith. It may be defined as a *positive conviction, wrought in the heart by the Holy Spirit, as to the truth of the gospel, and a hearty reliance on the promises of God in Christ.*

b. *The elements of faith.* We distinguish three elements in true saving faith. (1) *An intellectual element.* There is a positive recognition of the truth revealed in the Word of God, a spiritual insight which finds response in the heart of the sinner. It is an absolutely certain knowledge, based on the promises of God. While it need not be comprehensive, it should be sufficient to give the believer some idea of the fundamental truths of the gospel. (2) *An emotional element (assent).* This is not mentioned separately by the Heidelberg Catechism, because it is virtually included in the knowledge of saving faith. It is characteristic of this knowledge that it carries with it a strong conviction of the importance of its object, and this is assent. The truth grips the soul (3) *An element of the will (trust).* This is the crowning element of saving faith. It is a personal trust in Christ as Saviour and Lord, which includes a surrender of the soul as guilty and defiled to Christ, and a reliance on Him as the source of pardon and spiritual life. In the last analysis the object of saving faith is Jesus Christ and the promise of salvation in Him. *John* 3:16, 18, 36; 6:40; *Acts* 10:43; *Rom.* 3:22; *Gal.* 2:16. This faith is not of human origin, but is a gift of God, *1 Cor.* 12:8, 9; *Gal.* 5:22; *Eph.* 2:8. But its exercise is a human activity, to which the children of God are repeatedly exhorted, *Rom.* 10:9; *1 Cor.* 2:5; *Col.* 1:23; *1 Tim.* 1:5; 6.11.

c. *The assurance of faith.* Methodists maintain that he who believes is at once sure that he is a child of God, but that this does not mean that he is also certain of ultimate salvation, since he may fall from grace. The correct view is that true faith, including, as it does, trust in God, naturally carries with it a sense of safety and security, though this may vary in degree. This assurance is not the permanent conscious possession of the believer. He does not ever live the full-orbed life of faith, and as a result is not always conscious of his spiritual riches. He may be swayed by doubts and uncertainties, and is therefore urged to cultivate assurance, *2 Cor.* 13:5; *Heb.* 6:11; *2 Pet.* 1:10; *1 John* 3:19. It can be cultivated by prayer, by meditation on the promises of God and by the development of a truly Christian life.

To memorize. Passages showing:

a. *That God is the author of conversion:*
Acts 11:18. 'And when they heard these things, they held their peace, and glorified God, saying, Then to the Gentiles also hath God granted repentance unto life.'

2 Tim. 2:25. 'In meekness correcting them that oppose themselves; if peradventure God may give them repentance unto the knowledge of the truth.'

b. *That man co-operates in conversion:*
Isa. 55:7. 'Let the wicked forsake his way, and the unrighteous man his thoughts: and let him return unto Jehovah, and He will have mercy upon him; and to our God, for He will abundantly pardon.'

Acts 17.30. 'The times of ignorance therefore God overlooked; but now He commandeth men that they should all everywhere repent.'

c. *The necessity of conversion:*
Ezek. 33:11. 'Say unto them, As I live, saith the Lord Jehovah, I have no pleasure in the death of the wicked; but that the wicked turn from his way and live: turn ye, turn ye from your evil ways; for why will ye die, O house of Israel?'

Matt. 18:3. 'Verily I say unto you, Except ye turn, and become as little children, ye shall in no wise enter into the kingdom of heaven.'

d. *Historical faith:*

Acts 26:27, 28. 'King Agrippa, believest thou the prophets? I know that thou believest. And Agrippa said unto Paul, With but little persuasion thou wouldest fain make me a Christian.'

James 2:19. 'Thou believest that God is one; thou doest well; the demons also believe, and shudder.'

e. *Temporal faith:*

Matt. 13:20,21. 'And he that was sown upon the rocky places, this is he that heareth the word, and straightway with joy receiveth it; yet hath he not root in himself, but endureth for a while; and when tribulation or persecution ariseth because of the word, straightway he stumbleth.'

1 John 2:19. 'They went out from us but they were not of us; for if they had been of us, they would have continued with us: 'but they went out, that they might be made manifest that they all are not of us.'

f. *Miraculous faith:*

Matt. 17:20b. 'If ye have faith as a grain of mustard seed. ye shall say unto this mountain, Remove hence to yonder place: and it shall remove; and nothing shall be, impossible unto you.'

Acts 14:9, 10. 'The same heard Paul speaking: who fastening his eyes upon him, and seeing that he had faith to be made whole, said with a loud voice, Stand upright on thy feet. And he leaped up and walked.'

g. *Christ as the object of saving faith:*

John 3:16. 'For God so loved the world, that He gave His only begotten Son, that whosoever believeth on him should not perish, but have eternal life.'

John 6:40. 'For this is the will of my Father, that every one that beholdeth the Son, and believeth on Him, should have eternal life; and I will raise him up at the last day.'

h. *The necessity of cultivating assurance:*

Heb. 6:11. 'And we desire that each one of you may show the same diligence unto the fulness of hope even to the end.'

2 Pet. 1:10. 'Wherefore, brethren, give the more diligence to make your calling and election sure.'

For Further Study:

a.   What kind of repentance is mentioned in *Matt.* 27:3; *2 Cor.* 7:10b.

b.   Can you name biblical persons in whose lives conversion in the sense of an outstanding crisis could hardly be erected? See *Jer.* 1:4; *Luke* 1:5; *2 Tim.* 3:15.

c.   Can you name some of the great words of assurance found in the Bible? See *Heb.* 3:17, 18; *2 Cor.* 4:16–5:1; *2 Tim.* 1:12.

Questions for Review:

1.   In how many different senses does the Bible speak of conversion?
2.   How do temporary and repeated conversion differ?
3.   What is true conversion? What elements does it include?
4.   What elements are included in repentance?
5.   How do the Roman Catholics conceive of repentance?
6.   How does conversion differ from regeneration?
7.   Who is the author of conversion? Does man co-operate in it?
8.   Is conversion as a sharp crisis always necessary?
9.   Of how many different kinds of faith does the Bible speak?
10.   What is characteristic of historical, temporal, and miraculous faith?
11.   How does temporal faith differ from saving faith?
12.   What elements are included in faith? How much knowledge is needed?
13.   What is the crowning element of saving faith?
14.   Who is the object of saving faith?
15.   Does the Christian always have the assurance of salvation?
16.   How can he cultivate this assurance?

2 I

Justification

1.   THE NATURE AND ELEMENTS OF JUSTIFICATION. Justification way be defined as *that legal act of God by which He declares the sinner righteous on the basis of the perfect righteousness of Jesus Christ.* It is not an act or process of renewal, such as regeneration, conversion, or sanctification, and does not affect the condition but the state of the sinner. It differs from sanctification in several particulars. Justification takes place outside of the sinner in the tribunal of God, removes the guilt of sin, and is an act which is complete at once and for all time; while sanctification takes place in man, removes the pollution of sin, and is a continuous and lifelong process.

We distinguish two elements in justification, namely: (a) *The forgiveness of sins on the basis of the righteousness of Jesus Christ.* The pardon granted applies to all sins, past, present, and future, and therefore does not admit of repetition, *Psa.* 103:12; *Isa.* 44:22; *Rom.* 5:21; 8:1, 32–34; *Heb.* 10:14. This does not mean that we need no more pray for forgiveness, for the consciousness of guilt remains, creates a feeling of separation, and makes it necessary to seek repeatedly the comforting assurance of forgiveness, *Psa.* 25:7; 32:5; 51:1; *Matt.* 6:12; *James* 5:15; *1 John* 1:9. (b) *The adoption as children of God.* In justification God adopts believers as His children, that is, places them in the position of children and gives them all the rights of children, including the right to an eternal inheritance, *Rom.* 8:17; *1 Pet.* 1:4. This legal sonship of believers should be distinguished from their moral sonship through regeneration and sanctification. Both are indicated in the following passages: *John* 1:12, 13; *Rom.* 8:15,16; *Gal.* 4:5,6.

2.   THE TIME OF JUSTIFICATION. The word 'justification' is not always used in the same sense. Some even speak of a fourfold

justification: *a justification from eternity, a justification in the resurrection of Christ, a justification by faith,* and *a public justification in the final judgment.*

In explanation of this it may be said that in an ideal sense the righteousness of Christ is already accounted to believers in the counsel of redemption, and therefore from eternity, but this is not what the Bible means when it speaks of the justification of the sinner. We must distinguish between what was decreed in the eternal counsel of God and what is realized in the course of history.

Again, there is some reason for speaking of a justification in the resurrection of Christ. In a sense it may be said that the resurrection was the justification of Christ, and that in him the whole body of believers was justified. But this was a general and purely objective transaction, which should not be confused with the personal justification of the sinner.

When the Bible speaks of the justification of the sinner, it usually refers to the subjective and personal application and appropriation of the justifying grace of God. The usual representation is that we are justified by faith. This implies that it takes place at the time when we accept Christ by faith. Faith is called *the instrument* or *the appropriating organ* of justification. By faith man appropriates, that is, takes unto himself, the righteousness of Christ, on the basis of which he is justified before God. Faith justifies in so far as it takes possession of Christ. *Rom.* 4:5; *Gal.* 2:16. We should guard against the error of the Roman Catholics and the Arminians, that man is justified *on the basis* of his own inherent righteousness, or of his faith. Man's own righteousness or faith can never be the ground of his justification. This can be found only in the perfect righteousness of Jesus Christ, *Rom.* 3:24; 10:4; *2 Cor.* 5:21; *Phil.* 3:9.

3.   OBJECTIONS TO THE DOCTRINE OF JUSTIFIC-ATION. Various objections are raised to this doctrine. It is said that, if man is justified on the basis of the merits of Christ, he is not saved by grace. But justification, with all that it includes, is a gracious work of God. The gift of Christ, God's reckoning of His righteousness to us, and His dealing with sinners as righteous – it is all grace from start

to finish. Again, it is said to be unworthy of God to declare *sinners* righteous. But God does not declare that they are righteous in themselves, but that they are clothed with the righteousness of Jesus Christ. And, finally, it is said that this doctrine is apt to make people indifferent as to their moral life. If they are justified apart from any consideration of works, why should they care for personal piety? But justification lays the foundation for a living relationship with Christ, and this is the surest guarantee for a truly godly life. The man who is really in living union with Christ cannot be morally indifferent, *Rom.* 3:5–8.

To memorize. Passages speaking of:

a. *Justification in general:*
Rom. 3:24. 'Being justified freely by His grace through the redemption that is in Christ Jesus.'
2 Cor. 5:21. 'Him who knew no sin He made to be sin on our behalf; that we might become the righteousness of God in Him.'

b. *Justification by faith, not by works:*
Rom. 3:28. 'We reckon therefore that a man is justified by faith apart from the works of the law.'
Rom. 4:5. 'But to him that worketh not, but believeth on Him that justifieth the ungodly, his faith is reckoned for righteousness.'
Gal. 2:16. 'Yet knowing that a man is not justified by the works of the law but through faith in Jesus Christ, even we believed on Christ Jesus, that we might be justified by faith in Christ, and not by the works of the law: because by the works of the law shall no flesh be justified.'

c. *Justification and the forgiveness of sins:*
Psa. 32:1, 2. 'Blessed is he whose transgression is forgiven whose sin is covered. Blessed is the man unto whom Jehovah imputeth not iniquity, and in whose spirit there is no guile.'
Acts 13:38, 39. 'Be it known unto you therefore, brethren, that through this man is proclaimed unto you remission of sins; and by Him every

one that believeth is justified from all things, from which ye could not be justified by the law of Moses.'

d. *Adoption of children, heirs of eternal life:*

John 1:12. 'But as many as received Him, to them gave He the right to become children of God, even to them that believe on His name.'

Gal. 4:4, 5. 'But when the fulness of the time came, God sent forth His Son, born of a woman, born under the law, that He might redeem them that were under the law, that we might receive the adoption of sons.'

Rom. 8:17. 'And if children, then heirs; heirs of God, and joint heirs with Christ, if so be that we suffer with Him, that we may be also glorified with Him.'

e. *Justification based on the righteousness of Christ:*

Rom. 3:21, 22. 'But now apart from the law a righteousness of God hath been manifested, being witnessed by the law and the prophets; even the righteousness of God through faith in Jesus Christ unto all them that believe.'

Rom. 5:18. 'So then as through one trespass the judgment came unto all men to condemnation; even so through one act or righteousness the free gift came unto all men to justification of life.'

For Further Study:
a.   What fruits of justification are mentioned in *Rom.* 5:1–5?
b.   Does not James teach that man is justified by works? *James* 2:21–25.
c.   With what objection to the doctrine of justification does Paul deal in *Rom.* 3:5–8?

Questions for Review:
1.   What is justification?
2.   How does it differ from sanctification?
3.   What elements does it comprise?
4.   In how far are sins forgiven in justification?
5.   Why must believers still pray for forgiveness?

6. What is included in the adoption of citizen?
7. Can we speak of justification from eternity and in the resurrection of Christ?
8. How is faith related to justification?
9. What is the ground of justification? What is the Arminian view?
10. What objections are raised to this doctrine? Can you answer them?

22

Sanctification and Perseverance

The doctrine of justification naturally leads on to that of sanctification. The state of justification calls for a life of sanctification, consecrated to the service of God.

1.   NATURE AND CHARACTERISTICS OF SANCTIFI-CATION. Sanctification may be defined as *that gracious and continuous operation of the Holy Spirit by which He purifies the sinner, renews his whole nature in the image of God, and enables him to perform good works.* It differs from justification in that it takes place in the inner life of man, is not a legal but a recreative act, is usually a lengthy process, and never reaches perfection in this life. While it is very decidedly a supernatural work of God, the believer can and should co-operate in it by a diligent use of the means which God has placed at his disposal, *2 Cor.* 7:1; *Col.* 3:5–14; *1 Pet.* 1:22.

Sanctification does not consist in a mere drawing out of what is already given in regeneration, but serves to strengthen, to increase, and to fortify the new life. It consists of two parts: the gradual removal of the pollution and corruption of human nature, *Rom.* 6:6; *Gal.* 5:24, and the gradual development of the new life in consecration to God, *Rom.* 6:4, 5; *Col.* 2:12; 3:1, 2; *Gal.* 2:19. While it takes place in the heart of man, it naturally affects the whole life, *Rom.* 6:12; *1 Cor.* 6:15, 20; *1 Thess.* 5:23. The change in the inner man is bound to carry with it a change in the outer life. That man must co-operate in the work of sanctification follows from the repeated warnings against evils and temptations, *Rom.* 12:9,16,17; *1 Cor.* 6:9, 10; *Gal.* 5:16–23, and from the constant exhortations to holy living, *Mic.* 6:8; *John* 15:4–7; *Rom.* 8:12, 13; 12:1, 2; *Gal.* 6:7, 8, 15.

2.   THE IMPERFECT CHARACTER OF SANCTIFI-
CATION IN THIS LIFE. While sanctification affects every part of
man, yet the spiritual development of believers remains imperfect in this
life. They must contend with sin as long as they live, *1 Kings* 8:46; *Prov.*
20:9; *James* 3:2; *1 John* 1:8. Their lives are characterized by a constant
warfare between the flesh and the spirit, and even the best of them are
still confessing sin, *Job* 9:3, 20; *Psa.* 32:5; 130:3; *Prov.* 20:9; *Isa.* 64:6;
Dan. 9:7; *Rom.* 7:14; *1 John* 1:9, praying for forgiveness, *Psa.* 51:1, 2;
Dan. 9:16; *Matt.* 6:12, 13; *James* 5:15, and striving for greater perfection,
Rom. 7:7–26; *Gal.* 5:17; *Phil.* 3:12–14.

This truth is denied by the so-called Perfectionists, who maintain
that man can reach perfection in this life. They appeal to the fact that
the Bible commands believers to be perfect, *Matt.* 5:48; *1 Pet.* 1:16;
James 1:4, speaks of some as perfect, *Gen.* 6:9; *Job* 1:8; *1 Kings* 15:14;
Phil. 3:15, and declares that they who are born of God sin not, *1 John*
3:6, 8, 9; 5:18. But the fact that we must strive for perfection does not
prove that some are already perfect. Moreover, the word 'perfect' does
not always mean free from sin. Noah, Job, and Asa are called perfect,
but history clearly proves that they were not without sin. And John
evidently means either that the new man does not sin, or that believers
do not live in sin. He himself says that, if we say that we have no sin,
we deceive ourselves, and the truth is not in us. *1 John* 1:8.

3.   SANCTIFICATION AND GOOD WORKS. Sanctification
naturally leads to a life of good works. These may be called the fruits
of sanctification. Good works are not perfect works, but works that
spring from the principle of love to God or faith in Him, *Matt.* 7:17,
18; 12:33, 35; *Heb.* 11:6, that are done in conscious conformity to the
revealed will of God, *Deut.* 6:2; *1 Sam.* 15:22; *James* 2:8, and have as
their final aim the glory of God, *1 Cor.* 10:31; *Col.* 3:17, 23. Only they
who are regenerated by the Spirit of God can perform such good works.
This does not mean, however, that the unregenerate cannot do good
in any sense of the word. See *2 Kings* 10:29, 30; 12:2; 14:3; *Luke* 6:33;
Rom. 2:14. In virtue of the common grace of God they can perform
works that are in external conformity to the law and serve a laudable
purpose; but their works are always *radically* defective, because they are

divorced from the spiritual root of love to God, represent no real inner obedience to the law of God, and do not aim at the glory of God. In opposition to the Roman Catholics it should be maintained that the good works of believers are not meritorious, *Luke* 17:9, 10; *Eph.* 2:8–10; *Titus* 3:5, though God promises to reward them with a reward of free grace, *1 Cor.* 3:14; *Heb.* 11:26; and in opposition to the Antinomians the necessity of good works must be asserted, *Col.* 1:10; *2 Tim.* 2:21; *Titus* 2:14; *Heb.* 10:24.

4.   PERSEVERANCE OF THE SAINTS. The expression 'perseverance of the saints' naturally suggests a continuous activity of believers whereby they persevere in the way of salvation. As a matter of fact, however, the perseverance referred to is less an activity of believers than a work of God, in which believers must participate. Strictly speaking, the assurance of man's salvation lies in the fact that God perseveres.

Perseverance may be defined as *that continuous operation of the Holy Spirit in the believer, by which the work of divine grace that is begun inn the heart, is continued and brought to completion.* This doctrine is clearly taught in Scripture, *John* 10: 28, 29; *Rom.* 11:29; *Phil.* 1:6; *2 Thess.* 3:3; *2 Tim.* 1:12; 4:18. And it is only when we believe in this perseverance of God that we can in this life attain to the assurance of salvation, *Heb.* 3:14; 6:11; 10:22; *2 Pet.* 1:10. Outside of Reformed circles this doctrine finds no favour. It is said to be contradicted by Scripture which warns against apostasy, *Heb.* 2:1; 10:26, exhorts believers to continue in the way of salvation, *Matt.* 24:13; *Col.* 1:23; *Heb.* 3:14, and even records cases of apostasy, *1 Tim.* 1.19, 20; *2 Tim.* 2:17, 18; 4:10. Such warnings and exhortations would seem to assume the possibility of falling away, and such cases would seem to prove it completely. But as a matter of fact the warnings and exhortations prove only that God works mediately and wants man to co-operate in the work of perseverance; and there is no proof that the apostates mentioned were real believers. See *Rom.* 9:6; *1 John* 2:19; *Rev.* 3:1.

To memorize: Passages to prove:

a. *Sanctification as the work of God:*

1 Thess. 5:23. 'And the God of peace himself sanctify you wholly; and may your spirit and soul and body be preserved entire, without blame, at the coming of our Lord Jesus Christ.'

Heb. 2:11. 'For both He that sanctifieth and they that are sanctified are all of one: for which cause He is not ashamed to call them brethren.'

b. *Man's co-operation in sanctification:*
2 Cor. 7:1. 'Having therefore these promises, beloved, let us cleanse ourselves from all defilement of flesh and spirit, perfecting holiness in the fear of God.'

Heb. 12:14. 'Follow after peace with all men, and the sanctification without which no man shall see the Lord:'

c. *The mortification of the old man:*
Rom. 6:6. 'Knowing this, that our old man was crucified with Him, that the body of sin might be done away, that so we should no longer be in bondage to sin.'

Gal. 5:24: 'And they that are of Christ Jesus have crucified the flesh with the passions and the lusts thereof.'

d. *The quickening of the new man:*
Eph. 4:24. 'And put on the new man, that after God hath been created in righteousness and holiness of truth.'

Col. 3:10. 'And have put on the new man, that is being renewed unto knowledge after the image of Him that created him.'

e. *Sanctification incomplete in this life:*
Rom. 7:18. 'For I know that in me, that is, in my flesh, dwelleth no good thing: for to will is present with me, but to do that which is good is not.'

Phil. 3:12. 'Not that I have already obtained, or am already made perfect: but I press on, if so be that I may lay hold on that for which also I was laid hold on by Christ Jesus.'

f. *The nature of good works:*
1 Sam. 15:22. 'And Samuel said, Hath Jehovah as great delight in burnt-offerings and sacrifices, as in obeying the voice of Jehovah?

Behold, to obey is better than sacrifice, and to hearken than the fat of rams.'

1 Cor. 10:31. 'Whether therefore ye eat or drink, or whatsoever ye do, do all to the glory of God.'

Heb. 11:6. 'And without faith it is impossible to be well pleasing unto Him; for he that cometh to God must believe that He is, and that He is a rewarder of them that seek after Him.'

g. *Perseverance of the saints:*

John 10:28, 29. 'And I give unto them eternal life; and they shall never perish, and no one shall snatch them out of my hand. My Father, who hath given them unto me, is greater than all; and no one is able to snatch them out of the Fathers hand.'

2 Tim. 1:12. 'For which cause I suffer also these things: yet am I not ashamed; for I know Him whom I have believed, and I am persuaded that He is able to guard that which I have committed unto Him against that day.'

2 Tim 4:18. 'The Lord will deliver me from every evil work, and will save me unto His heavenly kingdom: to whom be the glory for over and ever.'

For Further Study:

a.   Can you infer anything from the following passages as to the time of complete sanctification? *Phil.* 3:21; *Heb.* 12:23; *Rev.* 14:5; 21:27.

b.   What parts of man does sanctification affect according to *Jer.* 31:34; *Phil.* 2:13; *Gal.* 5:24; *Heb.* 9:14?

c.   What does the word 'perfect' (for example, in the AV) mean in the following passages: *1 Cor.* 2:6; 3:1, 2; *Heb.* 5:14; *2 Tim.* 3:16?

Questions for Review:

1.   What is sanctification, and how does it differ from justification?

2.   Is it a work of God or of man?

3.   Of what two parts does sanctification consist?

4.   What proof is there that it is incomplete in this life?

5.   Who deny this and on what ground? How can you answer them?

6.　What are good works in the strict sense of the word?

7.　In how far can the unregenerate perform good works?

8.　Are good works meritorious or not? Are we not taught that they are rewarded?

9.　In what sense are good works necessary?

10.　What is meant by the perseverance of the saints?

11.　How can this doctrine be proved?

THE DOCTRINE OF THE CHURCH AND THE MEANS OF GRACE

23
Nature of the Church

1.   GENERAL DESCRIPTION OF THE CHURCH. The principal Old Testament word for 'church' is derived from a verb meaning 'to call', and the principal New Testament word, from a verb meaning 'to call out'. Both denote the church as an assembly called by God.

a. *Different meanings of the word in the New Testament.* Most generally it denotes a local church, whether assembled for worship or not, *Acts* 5:11; 11:26; *Rom.* 16:4; *1 Cor.* 11:18; 16:1. Sometimes it designates a domestic church, or 'the church in the house' of some individual, *Rom.* 16:5, 23; *1 Cor.* 16:19; *Col.* 4:15. In its most comprehensive sense it is a description of the whole body of believers, whether in heaven or on earth, *Eph.* 1:22; 3:10, 21; 5:23; *Col.* 1:18, 24.

b. *The essence of the church.* Roman Catholics and Protestants differ as to the essential nature of the church. The former finds this in the church as an external and visible organization, consisting primarily of the priest together with the higher orders of bishops, archbishops, cardinals, and the Pope. Protestants broke with this external conception and seek the essence of the church in the invisible and spiritual communion of the saints. The church in its essential nature includes the believers of all ages and no one else. It is the spiritual body of Jesus Christ, in which there is no place for unbelievers.

c. *Distinctions applied to the church.* In speaking of the church in general several distinctions come into consideration. (1) *The church militant and the church triumphant.* The church as she now exists on

123

earth is a militant church, that is called unto and is actually engaged in a holy war. The church in heaven on the other hand is the triumphant church, in which the sword is exchanged for the palm of victory. (2) *The visible and the invisible church.* This distinction applies to the church as it exists on earth, which is invisible as far as her spiritual nature is concerned, so that it is impossible to determine precisely who do and who do not belong to her, but becomes visible in the profession and conduct of its members, in the ministry of the Word and the sacraments, and in her external organization and government. (3) *The church as an organism and as an institution.* This distinction applies only to the visible church. As an organism it is visible in the communal life of believers and in their opposition to the world, and as an organization, in the offices, the administration of the Word and the sacraments, and in a certain form of church government.

d. *Definitions of the church.* The invisible church may be defined as *the company of the elect who are called by the Spirit of God, or simply, as the communion of believers.* And the visible church may be defined as *the community of those who profess the true faith together with their children.* It should be noticed that the membership in both is not altogether alike.

2.   THE ATTRIBUTES AND MARKS OF THE CHURCH.

There are especially three attributes of the church, and also three marks or external characteristics.

a. *Its attributes.* These are the following three: (1) *Its unity.* According to the Roman Catholics this is the unity of an imposing world-wide organization, but according to the Protestants, the unity of the spiritual body of Jesus Christ. (2) *Its holiness.* Roman Catholics find this in the holiness of its dogmas, its moral precepts, its worship, and its discipline; but Protestants locate it in the members of the church as holy in Christ and as holy in principle, in the possession of the new life, which is destined for perfect holiness. (3) *Its catholicity.* Rome lays special claim to this, because its church is scattered over the whole earth and has a greater number of members than all the sects taken together. Protestants claim that the invisible church is the real catholic church, because it includes all believers of all ages and all lands.

b. *Its marks or external characteristics.* While the attributes belong primarily to the invisible church, the marks belong to the visible church, and serve to distinguish the true from the false. These are also three in number. (1) *The true preaching of the Word of God.* This is the most important mark of the church, *1 John* 4:1–3; *2 John* 9. It does not mean that the preaching must be perfect and absolutely pure, but that it must be true to the fundamentals of the Christian religion, and must have a controlling influence on faith and practice. (2) *The right administration of the sacraments.* The sacraments may not be divorced from the Word, as in the Roman Catholic Church, and should be administered by lawful ministers, in accordance with the divine institution, and only to believers and their seed, *Matt.* 28:19; *Mark* 16:16; *Acts* 2:42; *1 Cor.* 11·23–30. (3) *The faithful exercise of discipline.* This is necessary for maintaining purity of doctrine and safeguarding the holiness of the sacraments. The Word of God insists on this, *Matt.* 18:18; *1 Cor.* 5: 1–5, 13; 14:33, 40; *Rev.* 2:14, 15, 20.

To memorize. Passages testifying to:

a. *The unity of the church:*

John 10:16. 'And other sheep I have, which are not of this fold: them also I must bring, and they shall hear my voice; and they shall become one flock, one shepherd.'

John 17:20, 21. 'Neither for these only do I pray, but for these also that believe on me through their word; that they may all be one.'

Eph. 4:4–6. 'There is one body and one Spirit, even as ye were called in one hope of your calling; one Lord, one faith, one baptism, one God and Father of all, who is over all, and through all, and in all.'

b. *The holiness of the church:*

Exod. 19:6. 'And ye shall be unto me a kingdom of priests, and a holy nation.'

1 Pet. 2:9. 'But ye are an elect race, a Royal priesthood, a holy nation, a people for God's own possession, that ye may show forth the excellencies of Him who called you out of darkness into His marvellous light.'

c. *The catholicity of the church:*

Psa. 2:8. 'Ask of me, and I will give thee the nations for thine inheritance, and the uttermost parts of the earth for thy possessions.'

Rev. 7:9. 'After these things I saw, and behold, a great multitude, which no man could number, out of every nation and of all tribes and peoples and tongues, standing before the throne and before the Lamb, arrayed in white robes, and palms in their hands.'

d. *The necessity of adhering to the truth:*

2 Tim. 1:13. 'Hold the pattern of sound words which thou hast heard from me, in faith and love which is in Christ Jesus.'

2 Tim. 2:15. 'Give diligence to present thyself approved unto God, a workman that needeth not to be ashamed, handling aright the word of truth.'

Titus 2:1. 'But speak thou the things which befit the sound doctrine.'

e. *The necessity of the right administration of the sacraments:*

Acts 19:4, 5. 'And Paul said, John baptised with the baptism of repentance, saying unto the people that they should believe on him that should come after him, that is, on Jesus. And when they heard this, they were baptized into the name of the Lord Jesus.'

1 Cor. 11:28–30. 'But let a man prove himself, and so let him eat of the bread, and drink of the cup. For he that eateth and drinketh, eateth and drinketh judgment unto himself, if he discern not the body. For this cause many among you are weak and sickly, and not a few sleep.'

f. *The necessity of discipline:*

Matt. 16:19. 'I will give unto thee the keys of the kingdom of heaven: and whatsoever thou shalt bind on earth shall be bound in heaven; and whatsoever thou shalt loose on earth shall be loosed in heaven.'

Titus 3:10, 11. 'A factious man after a first and second admonition refuse; knowing that such a one is perverted, and sinneth being self-condemned.'

For Further Study:

a.   Did the church exist before the day of Pentecost? See *Matt.* 18:17; *Acts* 7:38.

b.   Is the word 'church' ever used in the singular in the New Testament to denote a group of churches? See *Acts* 9:31.

c.   What causes for discipline were there in the Corinthian church? *1 Cor.* 5:1–5, 13; 11:17–34; *2 Cor.* 2:5–11.

Questions for Review:

1.   What is the meaning of the word 'church' in Scripture according to its derivation?
2.   What different meanings has the word in the New Testament?
3.   How do Roman Catholics and Protestants differ as to the essence of the church?
4.   What is the difference between the militant and the triumphant church?
5.   To what church does the distinction 'visible and invisible' apply?
6.   In what sense is the church called invisible?
7.   How does the church as an organism and as an institution differ?
8.   How can we defuse the invisible, and how the visible church?
9.   Which are the attributes of the church, and how does our conception of them differ from that of the Catholics?
10. Which are the marks of the church, and what purpose do they serve?
11. Do they belong to the invisible or to the visible church?
12. How must we conceive of the true preaching of the Word?
13. What belongs to the right administration of the sacraments?
14. Why is discipline necessary?

24

The Government and Power of the Church

Christ is the Head of the church and the source of all its authority, *Matt.* 23:10; *John* 13:13; *1 Cor.* 12:5; *Eph.* 1:20–23; 4:11, 12; 5:23, 24. He rules the church, not by force, but by His Word and Spirit. All human officers in the church are clothed with the authority of Christ and must submit to the control of His Word.

1.   THE OFFICERS OF THE CHURCH. The officers of the church mentioned in the New Testament are of two kinds:

a. *Extraordinary officers.* The most important of these were the apostles. In the strictest sense this name applies only to the Twelve chosen by Jesus and Paul, but it is also given to some apostolic men, *Acts* 14:4, 14; *1 Cor.* 9:5, 6; *2 Cor.* 8:23; *Gal.* 1:19. The apostles had certain special qualifications. They were directly called by Christ, *Gal.* 1:1, saw Christ after the resurrection, *1 Cor.* 9:1, were conscious of being inspired, *1 Cor.* 2:13, performed miracles, *2 Cor.* 12:12, and were richly blessed in their labours, *1 Cor.* 9:1. The New Testament also speaks of *prophets*, men specially gifted to speak for the edification of the church and occasionally predicting future things, *Acts* 11:28; 13:1, 2; 15:32; *Eph.* 4:11. And, finally, it also mentions *evangelists*, who assisted the apostles in their work, *Acts* 21:8; *Eph.* 4:11; *2 Tim.* 4:5.

b. *Ordinary officers.* Frequent mention is made of *elders*, especially in the Acts of the Apostles, *Acts* 11:30; 14:23; 15:2, 6, 22; 16:4; 20:17; 21:18. Alongside this term, the name 'bishop' was used to designate the same kind of officers, *Acts* 20:17, 28; *1 Tim.* 3:1; 5:17, 19; *Titus* 1:5, 7; *1 Pet.* 5:1, 2. While both names were applied to the same class of officers, the name 'elder' stressed their age, and the name 'bishop' their work as overseers. The elders were not originally *teachers*, but gradually the teaching function was connected with their office, *Eph.* 4:11; *1 Tim.* 5:17; *2 Tim.* 2:2. From *1 Tim.* 5:17 it appears that some elders simply ruled, while others also taught. In addition to these the New Testament also speaks of *deacons, Phil.* 1:1; *1 Tim.* 3:8, 10, 12. The prevailing opinion is that the institution of this office is recorded in *Acts* 6:1–6.

2.   THE ECCLESIASTICAL ASSEMBLIES. The Reformed churches have a number of governing bodies. Their relation to each other is marked by a careful gradation. They are known as consistory, classis, and synod. The consistory consists of the minister and the elders of the local church; the classis, of one minister and one elder of each local church within a certain district; and the synod, of an equal number of ministers and elders from each classis.

a. *The government of the local church.* The government of the local church is of a representative character. The minister and the elders, chosen by the people, form a council or consistory for the government of the church, *Acts* 14:23; 20:17; *Titus* 1:5. While the elders are chosen by the people, they do not receive their authority from the people, but directly from Jesus Christ, the Lord of the church. Every local church is a complete church, fully equipped to rule its own affairs. But since it affiliates with other churches on the basis of a common agreement, it is not entirely independent. The church order serves to guard the rights and interests of the local church, but also the collective rights and interests of the affiliated churches.

b. *The major assemblies.* When local churches affiliate to give greater expression to the unity of the church, major assemblies, such as classes and synods become necessary. The council of Jerusalem, described in *Acts* 15, partook of the nature of a major assembly. The immediate representatives of the people, who form the consistories, are themselves represented by a limited number in classes, and these in turn are represented in synods. Ecclesiastical assemblies should naturally deal only with church matters, matters of doctrine and morals, of church government and discipline. But even so major assemblies must limit themselves to matters which as to their nature belong to the province of a minor assembly, but for some reason cannot be settled there; and matters which as to their nature belong to the province of a major assembly, because they pertain to the churches in general. The decisions on major assemblies are not merely advisory, but authoritative, unless they are explicitly declared to be only advisory.

3.   THE POWER OF THE CHURCH. The power of the church is spiritual, because it is given by the Holy Spirit, *Acts* 20:28, is a manifestation of the power of the Spirit, *John* 20:22, 23, pertains exclusively to believers, *1 Cor.* 5:12, 13, and can be exercised only in a spiritual way, *2 Cor.* 10:4. It is also a purely ministerial power, which is derived from Christ and is exercised in His name. The power of the church is threefold:

a. *A dogmatic or teaching power.* The church is commissioned to guard the truth, to hand it on faithfully from generation to generation, and to defend it against all forces of unbelief, *1 Tim.* 1:3, 4; *2 Tim.* 1:13; *Titus* 1:9–11. It must preach the Word unceasingly among all the nations of the world, *Isa.* 3:10, 11; *2 Cor.* 5:20; *1 Tim.* 4:13; *2 Tim.* 2:15; 4:2; *Titus* 2:1–10, must draw up creeds and confessions, and must provide for the training of its future ministers, *2 Tim.* 2:2.

b. *A governing power.* God is a God of order, who desires that all things in the church be done decently and in order, *1 Cor.* 14:33, 40. For that reason He made provision for the proper regulation of the affairs of the church, and gave the church power to carry the laws of Christ into effect, *John* 21:15–17; *Acts* 20:28; *1 Pet.* 5:2. This also includes the power of discipline, *Matt.* 16:19; 18:18; *John* 20:23; *1 Cor.* 5:2, 7, 13; *2 Tim.* 3:14, 15; *1 Tim.* 1:20; *Titus* 3:10. The purpose of discipline in the church is twofold, namely, to carry into effect the law of Christ concerning the admission and exclusion of members, and to promote the spiritual education of the members of the church by securing their obedience to the laws of Christ. If there are diseased members, the church will first seek to effect a cure, but if this fails it will put away the diseased members. It deals with public sins even when there is no formal accusation, but in the case of private sins insists on the application of the rule laid down in *Matt.* 18:15–18.

c. *A power or ministry of mercy.* Christ sent out His disciples, not only to preach, but also to heal all manner of diseases, *Matt.* 10:1, 8; *Luke* 9:1, 2; 10:9, 17. And among the early Christians there were some who had the gift of healing, *1 Cor.* 12:9, 10, 28, 30. This special gift came to an end with the passing of the apostolic age. From that time on the ministry of mercy was largely limited to the church's care for the poor. The Lord hinted at this task in *Matt.* 26:11; *Mark* 14:7. The early church practised a sort of communion of goods, so that no one wanted the necessaries of life, *Acts* 4:34. Later on seven men were appointed to 'serve the tables', that is, to provide for a more equal distribution of what was brought for the poor, *Acts* 6:1–6. After that deacons are repeatedly mentioned, *Rom.* 16:1; *Phil.* 1:1; *1 Tim.* 3:8–12. Great emphasis is placed on giving or collecting for the poor, *Acts* 11:29; 20:35; *1 Cor.* 16:1, 2; *2 Cor.* 8:13–15; 9:1, 6, 7; *Gal.* 2:10; 6:10; *Eph.* 4:28; *1 Tim.* 5:10, 16; *James* 1:27; 2:15, 16; *1 John* 3:17.

To memorize: Passages proving:

a. *That Christ is the Head of the church:*
Eph. 1:22b, 23. 'And He gave Him to be Head over all things to the church, which is His body, the fulness of Him that filleth all in all.'
Col. 1:18. 'And He is the head of the body, the church, who is the beginning, the firstborn from the dead: that in all things He might have the pre-eminence.'

b. *The special marks of an apostle:*
1 Cor. 9:1, 2. 'Am I not free? am I not an apostle? have I not seen Jesus our Lord? are ye not my work in the Lord? If to others I am not an apostle, yet at least I am to you: for the seal of mine apostleship are ye in the Lord.'
2 Cor. 12:12. 'Truly the signs of an apostle were wrought among you in all patience, by signs and wonders and mighty works.'

c. *The office of elder or bishop:*
Acts 14:23. 'And when they had appointed for them elders in every

church and had prayed with fasting, they commended them to the Lord, on whom they had believed.'

1 Tim. 3:1. 'Faithful is the saying, If a man seeketh the office of a bishop he desireth a good work.'

Titus 1:5. 'For this cause left I thee in Crete, that thou shouldest set in order the things that were wanting, and appoint elders in every city, as I gave thee charge.'

d. *The teaching function of some elders:*

1 Tim. 5:17. 'Let the elders that rule well be counted worthy of double honour, especially those who labour in the word and in teaching.'

2 Tim. 2:2. 'And the things which thou hast heard from me among many witnesses, the same commit thou to faithful men, who shall be able to teach others also.'

e. *The office of deacon:*

1 Tim. 3:10. 'And let these also first be proved then let then serve as deacons, if they be blameless.'

f. *The spiritual nature of the elders' work:*

Acts 20:28. 'Take heed unto yourselves, and to all the flock, in which the Holy Spirit has made you bishops, to feed the church of the Lord which He purchased with His own blood.'

1 Pet. 5:2, 3. 'Tend the flock of God which is among you exercising the oversight, not of constraint, but willingly, according to the will of God; nor yet for filthy lucre, but of a ready mind; neither as lording it over the charge allotted to you, but making yourselves ensamples to the flock.'

g. *The power of discipline:*

Matt. 18:18. 'Verily I say unto you, what things soever ye bind on earth shall be bound in heaven; and what things soever ye shall loose on earth shall be loosed in heaven.'

John 20:23. 'Whose soever sins ye forgive, they are forgiven unto them; whose soever sins ye retain, they are retained.'

For Further Study:

a.   What men besides the Twelve and Paul are called apostles? *Acts* 14:4, 14; *1 Cor.* 9:5, 6; *2 Cor.* 8:23; *Gal.* 1:1 9.

b.   Who are called evangelists in the Bible? *Acts* 21:8; *2 Tim.* 4:5.

c.   What is the course of discipline in connection with private sins indicated in *Matt.* 18:15–17?

Questions for Review:

1.   Who is the Head of the church and by what standard does He rule?

2.   What extraordinary officers were there in the church?

3.   What were the characteristics of the apostles?

4.   What did the prophets and the evangelists do?

5.   Which were the ordinary officers?

6.   What other name was used for elders? Did they all teach?

7.   When was the office of deacon instituted?

8.   What ecclesiastical assemblies do we distinguish?

9.   In how far is the local church independent?

10.   Is there any Scripture warrant for major assemblies? Where?

11.   How are they constituted, and with what matters can they deal?

12.   Are their decisions merely advisory?

13.   What different kinds of power has the church? What does each include?

14.   What is the purpose of church discipline?

15.   What do we understand by the ministry of mercy in the church?

THE MEANS OF GRACE

25

The Word of God and the Sacraments in General

1. THE WORD OF GOD. The Word of God is the most important means of grace, though Catholics ascribe this honour to the sacraments.

a. *The Word and the Spirit.* While the term 'means of grace' can be used in a broader sense, it is here used as a designation of the means which the church is directed to employ. When we speak of the 'Word' here, we do not refer to the personal Word (the second Person in the Trinity, *John* 1:1 ff.), nor to the creative word of power, *Psa.* 33:6; but very specially to the Word of God as it is contained in Scripture and is preached to the church. *1 Pet.* 1:25. It is the Word of God's grace, and therefore the most important means of grace. While the emphasis falls on the Word as it is *preached,* it may also be brought to men in other ways: in the home and in the school, by means of conversation and religious literature. The Word is made effective as a means of grace only through the operation of the Holy Spirit. The Word alone is not sufficient to work faith and conversion, but is yet the necessary instrument. While the Holy Spirit can, He does not ordinarily work without the Word. The preaching of the Word is made fruitful by the operation of the Spirit.

b. *Two parts of the Word as a means of grace.* The Word as a means of grace consists of two parts, namely, *the law* and *the gospel.* The law as a means of grace first of all serves the purpose of bringing men under conviction of sin, *Rom.* 3:20, making him conscious of his inability to meet the demands of the law, and becoming his tutor to lead him to Christ, *Gal.* 3:24. In the second place it is also the rule of life for believers, reminding them of their duties and leading them in the way of life and salvation. The gospel is a clear representation of the way of salvation revealed in Jesus Christ. It exhorts the sinner to come to Christ in faith and repentance, and promises those who truly repent and believe all the blessings of salvation in the present and in the future. It is the power of God unto salvation for every one that believeth. *Rom.* 1:16; *1 Cor.* 1:18.

2.   THE SACRAMENTS IN GENERAL. The Word of God is complete as a means of grace, but the sacraments are not complete without the Word. This must be maintained over against the Roman Catholics, who teach that the sacraments contain all that is necessary unto salvation. The Word and the sacraments differ in the following particulars: (a) the Word is absolutely necessary, while the sacraments are not; (b) the Word serves to beget and to strengthen faith, while the sacraments can only strengthen it; and (c) the Word is for all the world, but the sacraments only for believers and their seed. The following points deserve attention:

a. *The parts of the sacraments.* Three parts must be distinguished in the sacraments, namely, (1) *The outward and visible sign.* Each one of the sacraments contains an external element. This consists of water in baptism, and of bread and wine in the Lord's Supper. One who receives merely this may be said to receive the sacrament, but does not receive the whole, nor the most important part of it. (2) *The inward spiritual grace signified.* A sign points to something that is signified, and this is the internal matter of the sacrament. It may be called righteousness of faith, *Rom.* 4:11, the forgiveness of sins, *Mark* 1:4; faith and repentance, *Mark* 1:4; 16:16, or communion with Christ in His death and resurrection, *Rom.* 6:3, 4; *Col.* 2:11, 12. (3) *The union between the sign and the thing signified.* This really constitutes the essence of the sacrament. Where the sacrament is received in faith, the grace of God accompanies it.

The following definition may be given of a sacrament. *A sacrament is a holy ordinance instituted by Christ in which, by sensible signs, the grace of God in Christ is represented, sealed, and applied to believers, and they, in turn, express their faith and obedience to God.*

b. *The number of the sacraments.* During the Old Testament there were just two sacraments, namely, circumcision and passover. The former was instituted in the days of Abraham, and the latter in the time of Moses. Both were bloody sacraments in harmony with the Old Testament dispensation. The church of the New Testament also has two sacraments, namely, baptism and the Lord's Supper, both of which are unbloody. After Christ has brought His perfect sacrifice, no more shedding of blood is needed. The church of Rome enlarged the number of sacraments in an unwarranted manner by adding confirmation, penance, orders, matrimony, and extreme unction.

c. *Old and New Testament sacraments compared.* The Church of Rome holds that there is an essential difference between the two: the former being merely typical, affecting only the legal standing of the recipient and not his spiritual condition and depending for their effectiveness on the faith of those who received them; and the latter working spiritual grace in the hearts of the recipients irrespective of their spiritual condition, merely in virtue of the sacramental action. As a matter of fact. however, there is no *essential difference*, *Rom.* 4:11; *1 Cor.* 5:7; 10:1–4; *Col.* 2:11. There are some dispensational differences, however: (1) The Old Testament sacraments had a national aspect in addition to their spiritual significance. (2) They pointed forward to the coming sacrifice of Christ, while those of the New Testament point back to the completed sacrifice. (3) They did not convey to the recipient as rich a measure of spiritual grace as do the sacraments of the New Testament.

To memorize. Passages pointing to:

a. *The Word as a means of grace:*
Rom. 10:17. 'So belief cometh of hearing and hearing by the word of Christ.'

1 Cor. 1:18. 'For the word of the cross is to them that perish foolishness; but unto us who are saved, it is the power of God.'

b. *The two fold function of the law:*
Rom. 3:20. 'Because by the words of the law shall no flesh be justified in His sight; for through the law cometh the knowledge of sin.'
Rom. 7:7. 'What shall we say then? Is the law sin? God forbid. Howbeit, I had not known sin, except through the law: for I had not known coveting, except the law had said, Thou shalt not covet.'
1 John 5:3. 'For this is the love of God, that we keep His commandments: and His commandments are not grievous.'

c. *The function of the gospel:*
Rom. 1:16. 'For I am not ashamed of the gospel: for it is the power of God unto salvation to every one that believeth; to the Jew first, and also to the Greek.'
1 Cor. 1:18. See above under a.

d. *The spiritual significance of the sacraments:*
Rom. 4:11. 'And he received the sign of circumcision, a seal of the righteousness of the faith which he had while he was in uncircumcision.'
1 Cor. 5:7. 'For our Passover also hath been sacrificed, even Christ.'
Col. 2:12. 'Having been buried with Him in baptism, wherein ye were also raised with Him through faith in the working of God, who raised Him from the dead.'
John 6:51. 'I am the living bread which came down out of heaven: if any man eat of this bread, he shall live for ever; yea and the bread which I will give is my flesh, for the life of the world.'

For Further Study:
a. Is the law also a rule of life for New Testament believers? *Matt.* 5:17–19; *Rom.* 13:10; *Eph.* 6:2; *James* 2:8–11; *1 John* 3:4; 5:3.
b. Can you prove that the sacraments are only for believers and their seed? *Gen.* 17:10; *Exod.* 12:43–45; *Mark* 16:16; *Acts* 2:39; *1 Cor.* 11:28–29.

c.   What dispute arose in the early church about circumcision? *Acts* 15; *Gal.* 2:3–9.

Questions for Review:
1.   What do we mean by the term 'means of grace'?
2.   What do we mean by 'the Word of God' as a means of grace?
3.   Why is the Word the most important means of grace?
4.   What is the relation between the Word and the Spirit?
5.   What is the function of the law as a means of grace?
6.   What is the function of the gospel?
7.   How are the sacraments related to the Word?
8.   How do Word and sacraments differ as means of grace?
9.   What is a sacrament?
10.   What are the component parts of a sacrament?
11.   What is the sign in each one of the sacraments?
12.   What is the thing signified in each?
13.   How are the sign and the thing signified related?
14.   How did the Old Testament sacraments differ from those of the New?

26

Christian Baptism

Christ instituted baptism after the resurrection, *Matt.* 28:19; *Mark* 16:16. He charged His disciples to baptize those who were made disciples 'into the name of the Father and of the Son and of the Holy Spirit', that is, into special relationship with the triune God. While He did not intend to prescribe a formula, the church chose the words of the institution, when it felt the need of one. The present formula was in use before the beginning of the second century. Protestants regard a baptism as legitimate which is administered by a duly accredited minister and in the name of the triune God, while Roman Catholics, who regard baptism as absolutely necessary unto salvation, permit its administration, in case the life of a child is in danger, also to others than priests, particularly to midwives.

1.   THE PROPER MODE OF BAPTISM. Baptists not only maintain that the proper mode of baptism is by immersion, but even assert that immersion belongs to the very essence of baptism. Baptism applied in any other way is not baptism at all. They hold that the fundamental idea of baptism is that of being buried and rising again with Christ, *Rom.* 6:3–6; *Col.* 2:12, and that this is symbolically indicated only by immersion. But Scripture clearly represents purification as the essential thing in the symbolism of baptism, *Ezek.* 36:25; *John* 3:25, 26; *Acts* 22:16; *Titus* 3:5; *Heb.* 10:22; *1 Pet.* 3:21. And this can be symbolized by sprinkling or pouring as well as by immersion, *Lev.* 14:7; *Num.* 8:7; *Ezek.* 36:25; *Heb.* 9:19–22; 10:22. Consequently the mode of baptism is quite immaterial: it may be administered by immersion, but also by pouring or sprinkling. But the Baptists have another argument, namely, that the New Testament

warrants only baptism by immersion. However, they fail to prove their point. Jesus did not prescribe a certain mode of baptism and the Bible never stresses any particular mode. The word (*baptizo*) employed by Jesus does not necessarily mean 'to immerse', but may also mean 'to purify by washing'. There is not a single case of baptism mentioned in the New Testament of which we are sure that it was baptism by immersion. It is very unlikely that the multitudes who flocked to John the Baptist and the three thousand who believed on the day of Pentecost were baptized in that way. Neither is it likely that this mode was applied in the cases mentioned in *Acts* 9:18; 10:47; 16:33, 34.

2.   THE PROPER SUBJECTS OF BAPTISM. There are two classes to whom baptism is applied, namely, adults and infants.

a. *Adult baptism.* Baptism is intended for believers and their seed. In the words of the institution Jesus undoubtedly had in mind primarily the baptism of adults, for it was only with these that the disciples could begin in their missionary labours. His instruction implies that baptism had to be preceded by a profession of faith, *Mark* 16:16. On the day of Pentecost those that received the word of Peter were baptized, *Acts* 2:41; see also *Acts* 8:37 (AV); 16:31–34. The church should require a profession of faith of all adults seeking baptism. When such a profession is made, this is accepted by the church at its face value, unless there are good reasons to doubt its sincerity.

b. *Infant baptism.* Baptists deny the right of infant baptism since children cannot exercise faith, and since the New Testament contains no command to baptize children and does not record a single instance of such baptism. Yet this does not prove it unbiblical. (1) *The scriptural basis for infant baptism.* Infant baptism is not based on a single passage of Scripture, but on a series of considerations. The covenant made with Abraham was primarily a spiritual covenant, though it also had a national aspect, *Rom.* 4:16–18; *Gal.* 3:8, 9, 14. This covenant is still in force and is essentially the same as the 'new covenant' of the present dispensation, *Rom.* 4:13–18; *Gal.* 3:15–18; *Heb.* 6:13–18. Children shared in the blessings of the covenant, received the sign of circumcision, and were reckoned as part or the congregation of Israel, *2 Chron.* 20:13; *Joel*

2:16. In the New Testament baptism is substituted for circumcision as the sign and seal of entrance into the covenant, *Acts* 2:39; *Col.* 2:11, 12. The 'new covenant' is represented in Scripture as more gracious than the old, *Isa.* 54:13; *Jer.* 31:34; *Heb.* 8:11, and therefore would hardly exclude children. This is also unlikely in view of such passages as *Matt.* 19:14; *Acts* 2:39; *1 Cor.* 7:14. Moreover, whole households were baptized and it is unlikely that these contained no children, *Acts* 16:15; 16:33; *1 Cor.* 1:16. (2) *The ground and operation of infant baptism.* In Reformed circles some hold that children are baptized on the ground of a presumptive regeneration, that is, on the assumption (not the assurance), that they are regenerated. Others take the position that they are baptized on the ground of the all-comprehensive covenant promise of God, which also includes the promise of regeneration. This view deserves preference. The covenant promise affords the only certain and objective ground for the baptism of infants. But if the question is raised, how infant baptism can function as a means of grace to strengthen spiritual life, the answer is that it can at the very moment of its administration strengthen the regenerate life, if already present in the child, and can strengthen faith later on when the significance of baptism is more clearly understood. Its operation is not necessarily limited to the very moment of its administration.

To memorize. Passages bearing on:

a. *The institution of baptism:*
Matt. 28:19. 'Go ye therefore, and make disciples of all the nations, baptizing them into the name of the Father and of the Son and of the Holy Spirit.'
Mark 16:15, 16. 'Go ye into all the world, and preach the gospel to the whole creation. He that believeth and is baptized shall be saved; but he that disbelieveth shall be condemned.'

b. *Baptism as a symbol of purification:*
Acts 22:16. 'And now why tarriest thou? Arise, and be baptized, and wash away thy sins, calling on His name.'
1 Pet. 3:21. 'Which also after a true likeness doth now save you, even baptism, not the putting away of the filth of the flesh, but the

interrogation of a good conscience toward God, through the resurrection of Jesus Christ.'

c. *The substitution of baptism for circumcision:*
Col. 2:11, 12. 'In whom ye were also circumcised with a circumcision not made with hands, in the putting off of the body of the flesh, in the circumcision of Christ; having been buried with him in baptism, wherein ye were also raised with him through faith in the working of God, who raised Him from the dead.'

d. *The permanent application of the covenant of Abraham:*
Rom. 4:16. 'For this cause it is of faith, that it may be according to grace; to the end that the promise may be sure to all the seed: not to that only which is of the law, but to that also which is of the faith of Abraham, who is the father of us all.'
Gal. 3:29. 'And if ye are Christ's then are ye Abraham's seed, heirs according to promise.'

e. *The inclusion of children in the New Testament church:*
Matt. 19:14. 'But Jesus said, Suffer the little children, and forbid them not, to come unto me; for to such belongeth the kingdom of heaven.'
Acts 2:39. 'For to you is the promise, and to your children, and to all that are afar off, even as many as the Lord our God shall call unto Him.'
1 Cor. 7:14. 'For the unbelieving husband is sanctified in the wife, and the unbelieving wife is sanctified in the brother: else were your children unclean; but now they are holy.'

For Further Study:
a.   Do the following passages prove that the disciples did not use the trinitarian formula in baptism? *Acts* 2:38; 8:16; 10:48; 19:5.
b.   How does the spiritual meaning of baptism compare with that of circumcision? Compare *Deut.* 30:6; *Jer.* 4:4 with *Acts* 2:38; 22:16.
c.   Can you prove that circumcision was abolished in the New Testament? *Acts* 15; *Gal.* 2:3; 5:2, 3; 6:12,13.

Questions for Review:

1. When did Christ institute baptism?
2. What is the meaning of baptism into the name of someone?
3. Were the words of Christ intended as a formula?
4. What do Baptists regard as the essential thing in the symbolism of baptism?
5. What is the essential thing in it?
6. Did Christ prescribe a certain mode of baptism?
7. Can the necessity of immersion be proved from Scripture?
8. Who are the proper administrators of baptism? What is Rome's view?
9. What is the condition of adult baptism?
10. How can infant baptism be proved from Scripture?
11. What views are there as to the ground of infant baptism?
12. Which should be preferred, and why?
13. How can infant baptism be a means of grace?

27
The Lord's Supper

The Lord's Supper was instituted at the time of the passover shortly before the death of Jesus, *Matt.* 26:26–29; *Mark* 14:22–25; *Luke* 22:19, 20; *1 Cor.* 11:23–25. The new sacrament was linked up with the central element in the paschal meal. The bread that was eaten with the lamb was consecrated to a new use, and so was the wine of the third cup, 'the cup of blessing'. The broken bread and the wine symbolize the Lord's broken body and shed blood; the physical eating and drinking of these point to a spiritual appropriation of the fruits of the sacrifice of Christ; and the whole sacrament is a constant reminder of His redemptive death.

1. THE LORD'S SUPPER AS A SIGN AND SEAL. Like every other sacrament, the Lord's Supper is first of all a sign. The sign includes not only the visible elements of bread and wine, but also their eating and drinking. It is a symbolical representation of the Lord's death, *1 Cor.* 11:26 and symbolizes the believer's participation in the crucified Christ and in the life and strength of the risen Lord. In addition to this, it is also an act of profession on the part of those who partake of it. They profess faith in Christ as their Saviour, and allegiance to them as their King.

But the Lord's Supper is more than a sign; it is also a seal, which is attached to the thing signified and is a pledge of its realization. It gives believing partakers the assurance that they are the objects of the great love of Christ revealed in His self-surrender to a bitter and shameful death; that all the promises of the covenant and all the riches of the gospel are theirs; and even that the blessings of salvation are theirs in actual possession.

2.   THE PRESENCE OF CHRIST IN THE LORD'S SUPPER.
The question as to the nature of the presence of Christ in the Lord's
Supper is one that has long been debated, and one on which there
is still considerable difference of opinion. Four views come into consideration here.

a. *The view of Rome*. The church of Rome conceives of the presence
of Christ in the Lord's Supper in a *physical sense*. On the ground of
Jesus' statement, 'This is my body,' it holds that bread and wine change
into the body and blood of Christ, though they continue to look and
taste like bread and wine. This view is open to several objections: (1)
Jesus, standing before the disciples in the flesh, could not very well
say that He had His body in His hand; (2) Scripture speaks of the
bread as bread even after the supposed change has taken place, *1 Cor.*
10:17; 11:26–28; and (3) It is contrary to common sense to believe
that what looks and smells and tastes like bread and wine is indeed
flesh and blood.

b. *The Lutheran view*. Lutherans maintain that, while bread and wine
remain what they are, the whole person of Christ, body and blood,
is present *in, under,* and *along with*, the elements. When Christ had
the bread in His hand, He held His body along with it, and therefore
could say, 'this is my body.' Every one who receives the bread also
receives the body, whether he be a believer or not. This is no great
improvement on the Roman Catholic doctrine. It ascribes to Jesus'
words the unnatural meaning 'this accompanies my body'. Moreover,
it is burdened with the impossible notion that the body of Christ is
omnipresent.

c. *The Zwinglian view*. Zwingli denied the bodily presence of Christ
in the Lord's Supper, while admitting that He is spiritually present in
the faith of believers. For him the Lord's Supper was mainly a mere
sign or symbol, a memorial of the death of Christ, and an act of profession on the part of believers. Some of his statements, however, seem to
indicate that he also regarded it as a seal or pledge of what God does
for the believer in Christ.

d. *Calvin's view*. Calvin took an intermediate position. Instead of
the physical and local, he taught the spiritual presence of Christ in
the Lord's Supper. In distinction from Zwingli he stressed the deeper

significance of the sacrament. He saw in it a seal and pledge of what God does for believers rather than a pledge of their consecration to God. The virtues and effects of the sacrifice of Christ on the cross are present and actually conveyed to believers by the power of the Holy Spirit.

3. THE PERSONS FOR WHOM THE LORD'S SUPPER IS INSTITUTED. The Lord's Supper was not instituted for all indiscriminately, but only for believers, who understand its spiritual significance. Children, who have not yet come to years of discretion, are not fit to partake of it. Even true believers may be in such a spiritual condition that they cannot worthily take their place at the table of the Lord, and should therefore examine themselves carefully, *1 Cor.* 11:28–32. Unbelievers are naturally excluded from the Lord's Supper. The grace that is received in the sacrament does not differ in kind from that which is received through the instrumentality of the Word. The sacrament merely adds to the effectiveness of the Word and to the measure of the grace received. The enjoyment of its spiritual benefits depends on the faith of the participant.

To memorize. Passages bearing on:

a. *The institution of the Lord's Supper:*
1 Cor. 11:23–27. 'For I received of the Lord that which also I delivered unto you, that the Lord Jesus in the night in which He was betrayed took bread; and when He had given thanks, He brake it, and said, This is my body, which is for you: this do in remembrance of me. In like manner also the cup, after supper, saying, This cup is the new covenant in my blood: this do, as often as ye drink it, in remembrance of me. For as often as ye eat this bread, and drink the cup, ye proclaim the Lord's death till He come.'

b. *The Lord's Supper as a sign and seal:*
Matt. 26:26, 27. 'And as they were eating, Jesus took bread, and blessed, and brake it; and He gave to the disciples, and said, Take, eat, this is my body. And He took a cup and gave thanks and gave to them saying, Drink ye all of it; for this is my blood of the covenant, which is poured out for many unto the remission of sins.'

1 Cor. 10:16. 'This cup of blessing which we bless, is it not a communion of the blood of Christ? The bread which we break, is it not a communion of the body of Christ?'

c. *The Lord's Supper as an act of profession:*
1 Cor. 11:26. 'For as often as ye eat this bread, and drink the cup, ye proclaim the Lord's death till He come.'

d. *Worthy participation and self-examination:*
1 Cor. 11:27–29. 'Wherefore whosoever shall eat the bread or drink the cup of the Lord in an unworthy manner, shall be guilty of the body and the blood of the Lord. But let a man prove himself, and so let him eat of the bread, and drink of the cup. For he that eateth and drinketh, eateth and drinketh judgment unto himself, if he discern not the body.'

For Further Study:
a.   Do the words of Jesus in *John* 6:48–58 have reference to the Lord's Supper?
b.   Does the expression 'breaking bread' necessarily refer to the Lord's Supper? See *Acts* 2:42; 20:7, 11; 27:35; *1 Cor.* 10:16.
c.   Can you mention other cases in which the verb 'to be' cannot be taken literally? *John* 10:7; 11:25; 14:6; 15:1.

Questions for Review:
1.   What belongs to the sign in the Lord's Supper?
2.   What does the sacrament signify and what does it seal?
3.   What is the Roman Catholic view of the presence of Christ in the Lord's Supper?
4.   How do the Lutherans conceive of it?
5.   What objections are there to these views?
6.   What is the Zwinglian conception of the Lord's Supper?
7.   How does Calvin's conception differ from it?
8.   How does Calvin conceive of the Lord's presence in it?
9.   How does the grace received in the sacrament differ from that received through the Word?
10.   For whom was the Lord's Supper instituted?
11.   Who should be excluded form the table of the Lord?

THE DOCTRINE OF THE LAST THINGS

28

Physical Death and the Intermediate State

1. PHYSICAL DEATH. Physical death is variously represented in Scripture. It is spoken of as the death of the body, as distinguished from that of the soul, *Matt.* 10:28; *Luke* 12:4, as the termination or loss of animal life, *Luke* 6:9; *John* 12:25, and as a separation of body and soul, *Eccles.* 12:7; *James* 2:26. It is never an annihilation, but may be described as *a termination of physical life by the separation of body and soul.* Pelagians and Socinians teach that man was created so that he had to die, but this is not in harmony with Scripture. It teaches us that death resulted from sin and is a punishment for sin, *Gen.* 2:17; 3:19; *Rom.* 5:12, 17; 6:23. Instead of being something natural, it is an expression of divine anger, *Psa.* 90:7, 11, a judgment, *Rom.* 1:32, a condemnation, *Rom.* 5:16, and a curse, *Gal.* 3.13, filling the hearts of men with dread and fear.

But since death is a punishment for sin, and believers are redeemed from the guilt of sin, the question naturally arises, Why must they still die? It is clear that it cannot be a punishment for them, but must be regarded as an important element in the process of sanctification. It is the consummation of their dying unto sin.

2. THE INTERMEDIATE STATE. Opinions differ very much as to the condition of man between death and the general resurrection. The most important theories call for a brief discussion.

a. *The modern idea of sheol-hades.* The idea is very prevalent at present that at death both the pious and the wicked descend into an intermediate place, which the Old Testament calls *sheol*, and the New Testament, *hades*. It is not a place of reward or punishment, but a place where all share the same fate, a dreary abode where life is but a weakened reflection of life on earth, a place of weakened consciousness, of slumbrous inactivity, where life has lost its interests and the joys of living are turned into sadness.

But this is hardly a scriptural representation. If the terms *sheol* and *hades* always denote a place to which both the pious and the wicked descend, how can the descent into it be held up as a warning to the wicked, *Psa.* 9:17; *Prov.* 5:5; 7:27; 9:18; 15:24; 23:14? And how can Scripture speak of God's anger as burning there, *Deut.* 32:22? It was in *hades* that the rich man lifted up his eyes, *Luke* 16:23, and he calls it a 'place of torment,' verse 28. It is better to assume that the words *sheol* and *hades* are not always used in the same sense, but sometimes denote the grave, *Gen.* 42:38; *Psa.* 16:10, sometimes the state or condition of death, represented as a place, *1 Sam.* 2:6; *Psa.* 89:48, and sometimes the place of eternal punishment, *Deut.* 32:22; *Psa.* 9:17; *Prov.* 9:18.

b. *Purgatory, Limbus Patrum, and Limbus Infantum.* According to the Church of Rome the souls of those who are perfect at death are at once admitted to heaven, *Matt.* 25:46; *Phil.* 1:23, but those who are not perfectly cleansed at death – and this is the condition of most believers – enter a place of purification called purgatory. The length of their stay there varies according to the need of individual cases, and can be shortened by the prayers, good works, and masses of pious friends or relatives. This doctrine finds no support in Scripture. – The *Limbus Patrum* is the place where, according to Rome, the Old Testament saints were detained until Christ set them free between His death and resurrection. – And the *Limbus Infantum* is the supposed abode of all unbaptized children. They remain there without any hope of deliverance, suffering no positive punishment indeed, but excluded from the blessings of heaven. Neither of these views finds any support in Scripture.

c. *The sleep of the soul.* The notion that at death the soul enters into a state of unconscious repose or sleep, was advocated by several sects in the past, and is now also a favourite doctrine of the Irvingites in England and of the Russellites [Jehovah's Witnesses] in America. It has a peculiar fascination for those who find it hard to believe in a continuance of consciousness apart from the brain. They find support for it in Scripture passages which speak of death as a sleep, *Matt.* 9:24; *Acts* 7:60; *1 Thess.* 4:13, or seem to say that the dead are unconscious, *Psa.* 6:5; 30:9; 115:17; 146:4. But the former simply speak of death as a sleep because of the similarity between a dead body and a body asleep, and the latter simply stress the fact that the dead can no more take notice of nor share in the activities of the present world. Believers are represented as enjoying a conscious life immediately after death, *Luke* 16:19–31; 23:43; *2 Cor.* 5:8; *Phil.* 1:23; *Rev.* 6:9.

d. *Annihilationism and conditional immortality.* According to these doctrines there is no conscious existence, if any existence at all, of the wicked after death. Annhilationism teaches that man was created immortal, but that they who continue in sin are by a positive act of God deprived of immortality and finally destroyed or bereft forever of consciousness. According to the doctrine of conditional immortality, however, man was created mortal, and only believers receive the gift of immortality in Christ. The wicked ultimately perish completely or lose all consciousness. The result is the same in both cases. These doctrines are supposed to find support in the fact that the Bible represents eternal life as a gift of God in Christ, *John* 10:27, 28; *Rom.* 2:7; 6:23, and threatens sinners with death and destruction, *Psa.* 73:27; *Mal.* 4:1; *2 Pet.* 2:12. But the Bible clearly teaches that sinners will continue to exist, *Matt.* 25:46; *Rev.* 14:11; 20:10, and that there will be degrees of punishment of the wicked, *Luke* 12:47,48; *Rom.* 2:12.

e. *Second probation.* Some scholars hold that they who die in their sins will have another opportunity after death to accept Christ. No man will perish without having been offered a favourable opportunity to know and accept Jesus. They appeal to such passages as *Eph.* 4:8, 9; *1 Cor.* 15:24–28; *Phil.* 2:9–11; *Col.* 1:19, 20; *1 Pet.* 3:19; 4:6. But these do not prove the point. Moreover, Scripture represents the state of unbelievers after death as a fixed state, which cannot be altered, *Eccles.* 11:3; *Luke* 16:19–31; *John* 8:21, 24; *2 Pet.* 2:4, 9; *Jude* 7, 13. Their judgment depends on what they have done in the flesh, *Matt.* 7:22, 23; 10:32, 33; 25:34–46; *2 Cor.* 5: 9, 10; *2 Thess.* 1:8.

To memorize. Passages proving:

a. *That death is a punishment for sin:*
Rom. 5:12. 'Therefore, as through one man sin entered the world, and death through sin; and so death passed unto all men, for that all sinned.'
Rom. 6:23. 'For the wages of sin is death; but the free gift of God is eternal life in Christ Jesus our Lord.'

b. *That believers are victorious over death:*
1 Cor. 15:55–57. 'O death, where is thy victory? O death, where is thy sting? The sting of death is sin; and the power of sin is the law; but thanks be to God, who giveth us the victory through our Lord Jesus Christ.'

c. *That sheol-hades is in some cases a place of punishment:*
Psa. 9:17. 'The wicked shall be turned back unto sheol, even all the nations that forget God.'
Prov. 15:24. 'To the wise the way of life goeth upward, that he may depart from sheol beneath.'
Luke 16:23. 'And in hades he lifted up his eyes, being in torments.'

d. *That believers are with Christ immediately after death:*
2 Cor. 5:8. 'We are of good courage, I say, and are willing rather to be absent from the body, and to be at home with the Lord.'
Phil. 1:23. 'But I am in a strait betwixt the two, having the desire to depart and be with Christ; for it is very far better.'

e. *That unbelievers continue to exist after death:*
Matt. 25:46. 'And these shall go away into eternal punishment; but the righteous into eternal life.'

Luke 12:47, 48. 'And that servant, who knew his lord's will, and made not ready, nor did according to his will, shall be beaten with many stripes; but he that knew not, and did things worthy of stripes, shall be beaten with few stripes.'

Rev. 14:11. 'And the smoke of their torment goeth up for ever and ever; and they have no rest day and night they that worship the beast and his image, and whoso receiveth the mark of his name.'

f. *That there is no escape after death:*

Luke 16:26. 'And besides all this, between us and you there is a great gulf fixed, that they that would pass from hence to you may not be able, and that none may cross over from thence to us.'

2 Pet. 2:9. 'The Lord knoweth how to deliver the godly out of temptation, and to keep the unrighteous under punishment unto the day of judgment.'

For Further Study:

a. What do the following passages teach respecting death? *1 Cor.* 15:55–57; *2 Tim.* 1:10; *Heb.* 2:14; *Rev.* 1:18; 20:14.

b. Do you think the following passages support the doctrine of purgatory? *Isa.* 4:4; *Mic.* 7:8; *Zech.* 9:11; *Mal.* 3:2; *Matt.* 12:32; *1 Cor.* 3:13–15.

c. Does the word of Jesus to the dying thief on the cross fit in with the doctrine of the sleep of the soul? *Luke* 23:43.

Questions for Review:

1. How is physical death represented in Scripture?
2. How can you prove that death is not something natural?
3. What is the connection between sin and death?
4. Is death a punishment for believers? What purpose does it serve?
5. What is the modern idea of sheol-hades?
6. What objections are there to this theory?
7. What do these terms denote in Scripture?
8. How do the doctrines of annihilation and conditional immortality differ?
9. What is the supposed scriptural basis for these?

10. How can you disprove them?
11. What is the Roman Catholic doctrine of Purgatory, *Limbus Patrum*, and *Limbus Infantum*?
12. What is the doctrine of the sleep of the soul?
13. What is its supposed Scripture basis? How would you refute it?
14. What is the doctrine of second probation?
15. Does Scripture support or contradict this doctrine?

29

The Second Coming of Christ

The New Testament clearly teaches us that the first coming of Christ will be followed by a second. Jesus referred to His return more than once, *Matt.* 24:30, 25:19; 26:64; *John* 14:3; angels called attention to it at the ascension, *Acts* 1:11; and the Epistles speak of it repeatedly, *Phil.* 3:20; *1 Thess.* 4:15, 16; *2 Thess.* 1:7, 10; *Titus* 2:13; *Heb.* 9:28.

1. GREAT EVENTS PRECEDING THE SECOND COMING. According to Scripture several important events must precede the return of Christ.

a. *The calling of the Gentiles.* The gospel of the kingdom must be preached to all nations before the coming of Christ, *Matt.* 24:14; *Mark* 13:10; *Rom.* 11:25. This means that the nations as a whole must be so thoroughly evangelized that the gospel becomes a power in the life of the people, a sign that calls for decision.

b. *The conversion of the full number of Israel.* 2 *Cor.* 3:15 and *Rom.* 11:25–29 refer to a conversion of Israel, and the passage in Romans seems to connect this with the end of time. Some take these passages to teach that Israel as a whole, Israel as a nation, will finally turn to the Lord. It is more likely, however, that the expression 'all Israel' in *Rom.* 11:26 simply refers to the full number of the elect out of the ancient covenant people. The whole passage does seem to imply that in the end large numbers of Israel will turn to the Lord.

c. *The great apostasy and the great tribulation.* The Bible teaches repeatedly that toward the end of time there will be a great falling away. Iniquity will increase, and the love of many will wax cold, *Matt.* 24:12; *2 Thess.* 2:3; *2 Tim.* 3:1–7; 4:3, 4. Wickedness crying to high heaven will result in a terrible tribulation, 'such as hath not been from the beginning of the world until now, no, nor ever shall be.' *Matt.* 24:21. If those days were not shortened no flesh would be saved; but they will be shortened for the sake of the elect.

d. *The coming of Antichrist.* The spirit of Antichrist was already in evidence in the apostolic age, *1 John* 4:3, and many antichrists had made their appearance, *1 John* 2:15. But the Bible leads us to expect that at the end of the age a single individual will stand out as the incarnation of all wickedness, 'the man of sin,' 'the son of perdition, he that opposeth and exalteth himself against all that is called God or that is worshipped; so that he sitteth in the temple of God, setting himself forth as God.' *2 Thess.* 2:3, 4.

e. *Signs and wonders.* The Bible also refers to striking signs as marking the beginning of the end. There will be wars, famines, and earthquakes in diverse places which are called the beginning of travail, to be followed by the rebirth of the universe; and also fearful portents in heaven, when the powers of the heavens will be shaken, *Matt.* 24:29,30; *Mark* 13:24,25; *Luke* 21:25,26.

2.   THE SECOND COMING ITSELF. After these signs the Son of Man will be seen coming on the clouds of heaven.

a. *The time of His coming.* Some believe that the coming of Christ is imminent, that is, may now occur at any time. But the Bible teaches us that the events and signs mentioned in the foregoing must precede the return. From God's point of view the coming is always near, *Heb.* 10:25; *James* 5:9; *1 Pet.* 4:5; but no one can determine the exact time, not even the angels nor the Son of Man, *Matt.* 24:36.

b. *The manner of His coming.* The Person of Christ will return. He has already come in the Spirit on the day of Pentecost, but He will return in the body, so that He can be seen, *Matt.* 24:30; 26:64; *Acts* 1:11; *Titus* 2:13; *Rev.* 1:7. Though several signs will precede His coming, yet it will be unexpected and take people by surprise, *Matt.* 24:37–44; 25:1–12; *1 Thess.* 5:2, 3; *Rev.* 3:3. Moreover, it will be a glorious and triumphant coming. The clouds of heaven will be His chariot, *Matt.* 24:30, the angels His bodyguard, *2 Thess.* 1:7, the archangels His heralds, *1 Thess.* 4:16, and the saints of God His glorious retinue, *1 Thess.* 3:13; *2 Thess.* 1:10.

c. *The purpose of His coming.* Christ will return to introduce the future age, the eternal state of things, and will do this by two mighty events, the resurrection and the final judgment, *John* 5:25–29; *Acts* 17:31; *Rom.* 2:3–16; *2 Cor.* 5:10; *Phil.* 3:20, 21; *1 Thess.* 4:13–17; *2 Pet.* 3:10–13; *Rev.* 20:11–15; 22:12.

3.   THE QUESTION OF THE MILLENNIUM. Some believe that the second coming of Christ will either be preceded or followed by a millennium.

a. *Post-millennialism.* Post-millennialism teaches that the second coming of Christ will follow the millennium. The millennium is expected during the gospel dispensation, in which we are now living, and at the end of which Christ will appear. The expectation is that the gospel will in the end become much more effective than it is at present and will usher in a period of righteousness and peace and of rich spiritual blessings. In our days some even expect that this will be the grand result of a purely natural process of evolution. This whole idea, however, does not seem to fit in with what the Bible tells us respecting the great apostasy toward the end of time.

b. *Pre-millennialism.* According to Pre-millennialism Christ at His return will re-establish the kingdom of David on earth, and will reign at Jerusalem for a thousand years. This theory is based on a literalistic interpretation of the prophets and of *Rev.* 20:1–6. It makes the kingdom of God an earthly and national kingdom, while the New Testament represents it as spiritual and universal, a kingdom that is even now in existence, *Matt.* 11:12; 12:28; *Luke* 17:21; *John* 18:36, 37; *Col.* 1:13. The New Testament knows nothing of such an earthly and temporal kingdom of Christ, but does speak of His heavenly (*2 Tim.* 4:18) and eternal (*2 Pet.* 1:11) kingdom. Moreover, this theory seeks its main support in a passage (*Rev.* 20:1–6), which represents a scene in heaven, and makes no mention of the Jews, of an earthly and national kingdom, nor of the land of Palestine, as the place where Jesus will rule.

To memorize. Passages pertaining to:

a. *The calling of the Gentile:*
Matt. 24:14. 'And this gospel of the kingdom shall be preached in the whole world for a testimony unto all the nations; and then shall the end come.'
Rom. 11:25, 26a. 'For I would not, brethren, have you ignorant of this mystery, lest ye be wise in your own conceits, that a hardening in part hath befallen Israel, until the fulness of the Gentiles be come in; and so all Israel shall be saved.'

b. *The conversion of Israel:*
Rom. 11:26. See above under a.
2 Cor. 3:15, 16. 'But unto this day, whensoever Moses is read, a veil lieth upon their heart. But whensoever it shall turn to the Lord, the veil is taken away.'

c. *The great apostasy and the great tribulation:*
Matt. 24:9–13. 'Then they shall deliver you up unto tribulation, and shall kill you: and ye shall be hated of all the nations for my name's sake. And then shall many stumble and shall deliver up one another, and shall hate one another. And many false prophets shall arise, and shall lead many astray. And because iniquity shall be multiplied, the love of the many shall wax cold. But he that endureth to the end, the same shall be saved.'
Matt. 24:21, 22. 'For then shall be great tribulation, such as hath not been from the beginning of the world until now, no, nor ever shall be. And except those days had been shortened, no flesh would have been saved: but for the elect's sake those days shall be shortened.'

d. *The revelation of Antichrist:*
2 Thess. 2:8, 9. 'And then shall be revealed the lawless one, whom the Lord Jesus shall slay with the breath of His mouth, and bring to

nought by the manifestation of His coming; even he, whose coming is according to the working of Satan with all power and signs and lying wonders.'

1 John 2:18a, 22. 'Little children, it is the last hour; and as ye heard that antichrist cometh, even now have there arisen many antichrists . . . Who is the liar but he that denieth that Jesus is the Christ? This is the Antichrist, even he that denieth the Father and the Son.'

e. *The second coming of Christ:*

Matt. 24:44. 'Therefore be ye also ready; for in an hour that ye think not the Son of Man cometh.'

Phil. 3:20. 'For our citizenship is in heaven; whence also we wait for a Saviour, the Lord Jesus Christ.'

Titus 2:13. 'Looking for the blessed hope and appearing of the glory of the great God and our Saviour Jesus Christ.'

For Further Study:

a. How would you explain the passages that speak of the coming of Christ as near? *Matt.* 16:28; 24:34; *Heb.* 10: 25; *James* 5:9; *1 Pet.* 4:5; *1 John* 2:18.

b. Who are the 'false Christs' or 'antichrists,' of which the Bible speaks, *Matt.* 24:24; *1 John* 2:18?

c. What would you say in reply to the idea that the second coming of Christ belongs to the past, since He returned in the Spirit, *John* 14:18, 28?

Questions for Review:

1. What great events will precede the second coming of Christ?
2. In what sense must the nations be evangelized?
3. How must we understand the predicted conversion of Israel?
4. What is the great apostasy and the great tribulation?
5. What does the Bible mean when it speaks of the Antichrist?
6. In what sense are there antichrists even now?
7. What signs will precede the second coming?
8. In what sense can it be regarded as near?
9. Can we regard the second coming as a past event? If not, why not?

10. Can you prove that it will be physical and visible?
11. How can it be sudden, when it will be preceded by signs?
12. What will be the purpose of Christ's return?
13. What is the difference between post- and pre-millennialism?
14. What objections are there to these theories?

30

The Resurrection, the Last Judgment, and the Final State

1.   THE RESURRECTION. Scripture teaches us that at the return of Christ the dead will be raised up. The Old Testament clearly speaks of it in *Isa.* 26:19, *Dan.*12:2. The New Testament contains more abundant proof of it, *John* 5:25–29; 6:39, 40, 44; 11:24; *1 Cor.* 15; *1 Thess.* 4:13–17; *Rev.* 20:13.

a. *The character of the resurrection.* Scripture teaches us to look forward to a bodily resurrection, similar to the resurrection of Christ. The redemption in Christ will include the body, *Rom.* 8:23; *1 Cor.* 6:13–20. Such a resurrection is clearly taught in *1 Cor.* 15, and in *Rom.* 8. It will include both the righteous and the wicked, but will be an act of deliverance and glorification only for the former. For the latter the re-union of body and soul will issue in the extreme penalty of eternal death.

b. *The time of the resurrection.* According to Scripture the general resurrection will coincide with the return of Christ and the end of the world, and will immediately precede the final judgment, *John* 5:27–29; 6:39, 40, 44, 54; 11:24; *1 Cor.* 15:23; *Phil.* 3:20, 21; *Rev.* 20: 11–15. Pre-millennarians teach a double resurrection: one of the just at the return of Christ, and another of the unjust a thousand years later, at the end of the world. But the Bible speaks of the resurrection of both in a single breath. *Dan.* 12:2; *John* 5:28, 29; *Acts* 24:15. It connects the judgment of the wicked with the coming of Christ, *2 Thess.* 1: 7–10, and places the resurrection of the just at the last day, *John* 6:39, 40, 44, 54; 11:24.

2.   THE LAST JUDGMENT. The doctrine of the resurrection leads right on to that of the last judgment. The Bible speaks of the coming of a final judgment in no uncertain terms, *Psa.* 96:13; 98:9; *Eccles.* 3:17; 12:14; *Matt.* 25:31–46; *Rom.* 2:5–10; *2 Cor.* 5.10; *2 Tim.* 4:1; *1 Pet.* 4:5; *Rev.* 20:11–14.

a. *The Judge and His Assistants.* Christ as the Mediator will be the Judge, *Matt.* 25:31, 32; *John* 5:27; *Acts* 10:42; 17:31; *Phil.* 2:10; *1 Tim.* 4:1. This honour was conferred on Christ as a reward for His atoning work. The angels will assist Him, *Matt.* 13:41, 42; 24:31; 25:31, and the saints will also have some share in His judicial work, *1 Cor.* 6:2, 3; *Rev.* 20:4.

b. *The parties that will be judged.* It is perfectly evident from Scripture that every individual of the human race will have to appear before the judgment seat, *Eccles.* 12:14; *Matt.* 12:36, 37; 25:32; *Rom.* 14:10; *2 Cor.* 5:10; *Rev.* 20:12. Some think that the righteous will be excepted, but this is contrary to *Matt.* 13:30, 40–43, 49; 25:31–36; *2 Cor.* 5:10. Clearly the demons will also be judged, *Matt.* 8:29; *1 Cor.* 6:3; *2 Pet.* 2:4; *Jude* 6.

c. *The time of the judgment.* The final judgment will naturally be at the end of the world, and will follow immediately after the resurrection of the dead, *John* 5:28, 29; *Rev.* 20:12, 13. The duration of the judgment cannot be determined. The Bible speaks of 'the day of judgment', but this does not necessarily mean that it will be a day of twenty-four hours. Neither is there any ground to assert with the Pre-millennarians that it will be a day of a thousand years.

d. *The standard of judgment.* The standard by which saints and sinners will be judged will evidently be the revealed will of God. Gentiles will be judged by the law of nature; Jews by the Old Testament revelation, and those acquainted with the fuller revelation of the gospel will be judged by it, *Rom.* 2:12. God will give every man his due.

3.   THE FINAL STATE. The final Judgment serves the purpose of setting forth clearly what the final state of each person will be.

a. *The final state of the wicked.* The wicked are consigned to the place of punishment called 'hell'. Some deny that hell is a place and regard it merely as a condition, but the Bible uses local terms right along. It speaks, for instance, of a 'furnace of fire', *Matt.* 13:42, a 'lake of fire', *Rev.* 20:14, 15, and of a 'prison', *1 Pet.* 3:19, all of which are local terms. In this place they will be totally deprived of the divine favour, will experience an endless disturbance of life, will suffer positive pains in body and soul, and will be subject to pangs of conscience, anguish and despair, *Matt.* 8:12, 13; *Mark* 9:47, 48; *Luke* 16:23. 28; *Rev.* 14:10; 21:8. There will be degrees in their punishment, *Matt.* 11:22, 24; *Luke* 12:47, 48; 20:47. It is evident that their punishment will be eternal. Some deny this, because the words 'eternal' and 'everlasting' may simply denote a long period of time. Yet this is not the usual meaning of the words and there is no reason to think that they have that meaning when applied to the future punishment of the wicked. Moreover, other terms are used, which point to endless punishment, *Mark* 9: 43, 48; *Luke* 16:26.

b. *The final state of the righteous.* The final state of believers will be preceded by the passing of the present world and the establishment of a new creation. This will not be an entirely new creation, but rather a renewal of the present creation, *Psa.* 102:26, 27; *Heb.* 12:26–28. Heaven will be the eternal abode of believers. Some think of heaven merely as a condition, but the Bible clearly represents it as a place, *John* 14:2; *Matt.* 22:12, 13; 25:10–12. The righteous will not only inherit heaven, but the entire new creation, *Matt.* 5:5; *Rev.* 21:1–3. The reward of the righteous is described as eternal life, that is, not merely endless life, but life in all its fulness, without any of the imperfections and disturbances of the present. This fulness of life is enjoyed in communion with God, which is really the essence of eternal life, *Rev.* 21:3. While all will enjoy perfect bliss, there will be degrees also in the enjoyments of heaven, *Dan.* 12:3; *2 Cor.* 9:6.

To memorize. Passages proving:

a. *A general resurrection:*
Dan. 12:2. 'And many of them that sleep in the dust of the earth shall

awake, some to everlasting life, and some to shame and everlasting contempt.'

John 5:28, 29. 'Marvel not at this: for the hour cometh, in which all that are in the tombs shall hear His voice, and shall come forth; they that have done good, unto the resurrection of life; and they that have done evil, unto the resurrection of judgment.'

Acts 24:15. 'Having hope toward God, which these also themselves look for, that there shall be a resurrection both of the just and unjust.'

b. *A resurrection of the body:*

Rom. 8:11. 'But if the Spirit of Him that raised up Jesus from the dead dwelleth in you, He that raised up Christ Jesus from the dead shall give life also to your mortal bodies through His Spirit that dwelleth in you.'

1 Cor. 15:35. 'But some will say, How are the dead raised? and with what manner of body do they come?' Also verse 44. 'It is sown a natural body; it is raised a spiritual body.'

c. *A resurrection at the last day or at the coming of Christ:*

1 Cor. 15:22, 23. 'But as in Adam all die, so also in Christ shall all be made alive. But each in his own order: Christ the first fruits; then they that are Christ's at His coming.'

1 Thess. 4:16. 'For the Lord Himself shall descend from heaven with a shout, with the voice of the archangel and with the trump of God: and the dead in Christ shall rise first.'

John 6:40. 'For this is the will of my Father, that every one that beholdeth the Son, and believeth on Him, should have eternal life: and I will raise Him up at the last day.'

d. *A final judgment with Christ as Judge:*

2 Cor. 5:10. 'For we must all be made manifest before the judgment-seat of Christ; that each one may receive the things done in the body, according to what he hath done, whether it be good or bad.'

2 Tim. 4:1. 'I charge thee in the sight of God, and of Christ Jesus who shall judge the living and the dead.'

Rev. 20:12. 'And I saw the dead, the great and the small, standing before the throne; and the books were opened: and another book was opened, which is the book of life: and the dead were judged out of the things which were written in the books, according to their works.'

e. *Eternal rewards and punishments:*
Matt. 25:46. 'And these shall go away into eternal punishment; but the righteous into eternal life.'
Rom. 2:6–8. 'Who will render to every man according to his works: to them that by patience in well-doing seek for glory and honour and incorruption, eternal life: but unto them that are factious, and obey not the truth, but obey unrighteousness, shall be wrath and indignation.'
2 Thess. 1:9. 'Who shall suffer punishment, even eternal destruction from the face of the Lord and from the glory of His might.'

f. *Degrees in rewards and punishments:*
Dan. 12:3. 'And they that are wise shall shine as the brightness of the firmament; and they that turn many to righteousness as the stars forever and ever.'
Luke 12:47, 48. 'And that servant, who knew his lord's will, and made not ready, nor did according to his will, shall be beaten with many stripes; but he that knew not, and did things worthy of stripes, shall be beaten with few stripes.'
2 Cor. 9:6. 'But this I say, He that soweth sparingly shall reap also sparingly, and he that soweth bountifully shall reap also bountifully.'

For Further Study:
a.   How does Jesus argue the resurrection in *Matt.* 22:23–33?
b.   Does Paul in *2 Thess.* 1:7–10 place the judgment of the wicked a thousand years after the coming of Christ?
c.   Does *1 Cor.* 6:3 prove that the good angels will also be judged?

Questions for Review:
1.   How can you prove the resurrection of the body from the New Testament?
2.   What Bible proof is there for the resurrection of the wicked?

3.   How does their resurrection differ from that of the righteous?
4.   What does the Bible teach respecting the time of the resurrection?
5.   How would you disprove the doctrine of a double resurrection?
6.   What Scripture proof is there for a last judgment?
7.   Who will be the Judge, and who will assist Him?
8.   What parties will be judged?
9.   When will the last judgment be, and how long will it last?
10.   By what standard will men be judged?
11.   In what will the punishment of the wicked consist?
12.   How can you prove that it will be unending?
13.   Will the new creation be an entirely new creation?
14.   What will be the reward of the righteous?

ALSO AVAILABLE FROM
THE BANNER OF TRUTH
TRUST

From the author of
A Summary of Christian Doctrine:

Systematic Theology

Louis Berkhof's *Systematic Theology* was his *magnum opus*. Into it he poured the stores of the accumulated knowledge he had gained during a lifetime devoted to preparing men for the ministry. His loyalty to the well-defined lines of the Reformed faith, his concise and compact style, and his contemporary treatment make the work the most important twentieth-century compendium of Reformed theology.

'Thoroughly loyal to the Bible in its completeness . . . a reference to the textual index shows that well over 3,000 separate texts and passages of Scripture are referred to . . . the reader cannot fail to be helped to a deeper understanding of biblical truth. The Banner of Truth Trust has put us all very much in its debt.'

AUSTRALIAN CHURCH RECORD

ISBN 978 0 85151 056 9, 784 pp., clothbound (not available in the USA)

LOUIS BERKHOF (1873-1957) was born in the Netherlands and emigrated with his family to Grand Rapids, Mich., in 1882. After graduating from Calvin Theological Seminary he served in two pastorates in the Christian Reformed Church, as well as studying for two years at Princeton University. In 1906 he was appointed to the faculty of Calvin Seminary and became its President in 1931. Among his twenty-two books was his Systematic Theology, *which has gone through many editions and has been translated into several languages.*

The History of Christian Doctrines

The History of Christian Doctrines is a companion volume to Louis Berkhof's *Systematic Theology*, and contains the historical material to be used with that work. As the author points out in his Preface, if the historical background is ignored, Christian teaching becomes distorted. Ancient heresies, long rejected by the church, are repeated and brought forth as new discoveries. The lessons of the past are neglected, and those who lived and laboured then are despised as if they achieved very little. In his concise and clear style, Berkhof traces the development of the major doctrines: the Trinity, the Person and work of Christ, sin and grace, the atonement, the work of the Holy Spirit (including the church and the sacraments), and eschatology.

'An excellent work by an excellent teacher.'

CHURCH OF ENGLAND NEWSPAPER

'A truly great work, and one that promises to retain for a long time its place among the most valuable books in theology.'

EVANGELICAL QUARTERLY

ISBN 978 0 85151 005 7, 288 pp., clothbound (also available in Spanish: ISBN 978 0 85151 716 2, 360 pp., paperback).

For free illustrated catalogue please write to
THE BANNER OF TRUTH TRUST

3 Murrayfield Road, Edinburgh EH12 6EL UK

P O Box 621, Carlisle, Philadelphia 17013, USA

www.banneroftruth.co.uk